THE CY   E

A RATIONAL EXPLANATION
FOR ASTROLOGY AND NUMEROLOGY

JOHN TATLER

PRISM · UNITY

For our survival
if we cannot seize the director's baton
to the orchestra of our affairs
we must at least know the tune that is playing

Published in Great Britain 1990 by:
PRISM PRESS
2 South Street,
Bridport,
Dorset DT6 3NQ

and distributed in the USA by:
AVERY PUBLISHING GROUP INC.,
120 Old Broadway,
Garden City Park,
New York 11040

and published in Australia 1990 by:
UNITY PRESS,
6a Ortona Road,
Lindfield,
NSW 2070

ISBN 1 85327 044 X

© 1989 John Tatler

Printed and bound in the Channel Islands
by The Guernsey Press Company Limited.

Contents

THE CYCLES OF TIME

Preface

Since the completion of this book it has been brought to my attention that I am by no means the first person to be aware of the relationship between astrology and cycles. Apparently there is an anonymous group of astrologers, an elite if you like, that felt it was proper and responsible to withhold this information. I have been told that they felt that the release of information of this type would have an undesirable result, and so decided that it was in the interests of all that it not be disclosed.

My answer is to state that the issues are much more than any adverse effect on a science that has survived for thousands of years. Astrology has survived much greater onslaughts than this book, in fact the efforts of astrologers through the centuries are vindicated by this book. This book is not intended as any vehicle of destruction, on the contrary. The purpose of this book is threefold:

1. To identify and demonstrate that cycles are not only statistical but predictive, to show that the human race is being directed onwards into time by unseen forces. To demonstrate that our free wills are not so free as we thought they were. This is the primary objective, a moral responsibility if you like. The existence or not of astrology and numerology is very much a secondary consideration.

2. To once and for all lay to rest any connection between astrology and magic. To vindicate all those lost and persecuted souls of the past that had faith in what they believed, yet paid the price for it.

3. To restate those words of Pythagoras that run through the very core of this book. Words that by their very simplicity are often overlooked, yet words that speak volumes of truth.

> *Evolution is the law of life.*
> *Number is the law of the Universe.*
> *Unity is the law of God.*

John Tatler

Introduction

O world invisible, we view thee,
O world intangible, we touch thee,
O world unknowable, we know thee,
Inapprehensible, we clutch thee!

Does the fish soar to find the ocean,
The eagle plunge to find the air —
That we ask of the stars in motion
If they have rumour of thee there?

Not where the wheeling systems darken,
And our benumbed conceiving soars! —
The drift of pinions, would we hearken,
Beats at our own clay-shuttered doors.

The angels keep their ancient places; —
Turn but a stone a start a wing'
'Tis ye, 'tis your estranged faces,
That miss the many-splendoured thing.

Francis Thompson

It was a warm, soft evening, the air was heavy with a faint scent of jasmine and all was still calm.

John stood on the balcony, his arm about Marcia's shoulders. They gazed up at the sky above them, there was not a cloud, the Moon was nearly full, shining brightly against the backdrop of stars. Stars that glistened like diamonds in the velvet blackness of space.

'Do you know', he said softly, 'Do you know that there are more stars in the sky than there are grains of sand in all the beaches of the world?'

Marcia looked up at him, snuggled close, smiled, and said 'Yes, I have heard that said', then after a pause, 'Do you believe in astrology?'

'Yes I do', his voice was firm, 'Why?'

'Because it fits, it works.'

'Oh.'

'Do you?'

We will return to Marcia and John later on. Their conversation was one that lovers and others must have had millions of times over the centuries, yet we are still no nearer to a conclusive answer to the question — Does astrology work?

When Sir Isaac Newton was challenged by Sir John Halley, about his belief in astrology he said, 'Sir, I have studied the subject, you have not.'

This book is about the question — Why? Why does astrology work and why does numerology work? What are the common factors between the two? Are there other clues to this mystery, this enigma of the ages?

In the beginning

Five thousand million years ago a great, whirling cloud of cosmic gas collapsed, the enormous forces at the nucleus forming a new star. This great, spinning cosmic cloud was the beginning of the solar system, for as the gas whirled on its axis, nine great masses of cosmic matter were hurled out into space to form the planets.

Nine planets that were to orbit the new Sun in a disk formation, a formation we call the ecliptic.

Since his genesis Man has created a symbolism of the planets, a heritage rich in his invention. An invention which we have come to know as Astrology.

Throughout time the astrologer has evolved a science that tells Man more about himself than he himself was aware of, it predicts the future with compelling accuracy, it lends understanding where understanding seems impossible. So it was that Astrology was labelled occult, so it was that it was connected with magic and superstition.

Astrology became the flagship of the occult, and the guns of the opposing fleet — the church and conventional science — were always trained on its rigging. Yet it survived for nearly six thousand years, and sailed on down through the centuries creating a symbolism, and evolving a system of interpreting the heavens that nobody has been able satisfactorily to explain.

Astrologers have ever sought that answer to silence their critics, yet no solution seemed forthcoming. The reason? Because astrologers did not look outside the boundaries of astrology with their question. They did not seek to find out why other phenomena should also work. For the key is outside these boundaries, the explanation is in time itself. In other words Astrology is a misconception, a cosmic red herring.

Let's go back to Marcia and John for a moment:

Marcia held John's hand tightly as they looked at the stars.

'John,' she said quietly, 'what do you mean astrology works?'

'I mean just that it works, it fits. What astrology says about someone is right, it's correct. Carl Jung said all the psychological knowledge since antiquity is in astrology, I believe him.'

'But how can this be so, how can all that knowledge be out there in the stars, just for us to read?'

'I don't believe it is, I believe we have just made it that way. I believe the answer lies in time.'

'In time, what do you mean in time?'

'I mean that we have made ourselves think the answer is out there in the stars for all to see, but in reality it was man looking for signs in the sky, to account for events that had happened, that ultimately caused him to fool himself.'

'I'm not sure I know what you mean.'

'Look, do you believe in astrology?'

'Yes, I think so.'

'Right, do you believe in numerology?'

'Yes I know that works.'

'Right, what is the common factor between the two?'

'I'm not sure — the date of birth?'

'Right, but it is not the date, because astrology converts it back to GMT and then to sidereal time. No the common factor is not the date but the moment of time.'

'The moment in time?'

'Yes, that's right, the moment in time. I have a theory about it. I think I might write a book.'

'Let me see if I understand you. You mean that if astrology works, and if numerology works, and the common factor is the moment in time, then the real thing that we should be looking at is not astrology or numerology but time.'

'Yes that's precisely what I mean.'

'But how was it that man came to fool himself?'

'Ah! that is the sixty-four dollar question, how was it, or rather why was it that man could fool himself? The answer to that, I think, is in the word assume.'

'Assume?'

'Yes, you've heard the old story about assume.'

'No.'

'Assume means to make an 'ass' of 'u' and 'me'.'

'Oh, very clever, would you get on with it.'

'OK, Man in the past, like you now probably, assumed that things just happened, one thing just followed another, and there was little pattern to it all. Do you not think it is like that?'

'Yeeess — somewhat.'

'Well, until comparatively recently, the 1930's to be exact, mankind would have been of that impression. However since the 1930's we have been aware that things go in cycles. All things — wars, our going to church, the stockmarket, wildlife — you name it, it goes in cycles!'

'Really?'

'Yes, these cycles have been going on for thousands of years, long before man got interested in astrology. So when he noticed an event, a war, a plague or whatever, he looked to the stars for confirmation.'

'So?'

'Well he always, or nearly always would have found it. The stars are nothing more than a moving map of time, a gigantic clock in the sky. But this clock does not measure minutes and seconds, it measures years and centuries. Look for a time period in the sky, and I guarantee that somewhere in the placings of the planets and stars you will find it.'

'And?'

'Well, man found the event in the sky that coincided with the event on earth, and assumed that it was the event in the sky that had signified the event on earth.'

'And that is how you think astrology came about?'

'Yes, that is roughly what I think.'

'Wait a minute, you have just said that man was wrong about what he thought was astrology.'

'Yes.'

'So how can you say that astrology works?'

'Because it is only how astrology is worked out, how it is calculated, that changes. The symbology and the interpretations do not change, they cannot change, they are the psychology of antiquity, they are only what man has learned about himself.'

'Oh! I think I see what you mean, but it is all so very complicated — kiss me.'

At that point I think we might leave Marcia and John.

Cycles are the scheme of things, cycles are like unseen currents in the river of life, a river of life flowing on into the future. Nature in all its aspects moves in cycles, from the tree, to the lowly grasshopper, to man himself, all operate in cycles. Cycles can be microscopic or cosmic, tangible or abstract, a millisecond or a millennium. When one is brought face to face with the fact that they seem to congregate in groups, and those groups exhibit a uniform timing, a synchronism, then the idea is staggering, the concept overwhelming.

For this book will demonstrate a connection between sunspots and the price of pig iron, an association between the orbit of Saturn and the cycle of economic depressions, a link between the orbit of Jupiter and stock market prices. It will show that there are cycles of the intangible, cycles of the emotions, cycles of personality. Moreover it will demonstrate a connection between these phenomena and the orbits of the planets.

The phenomena of cycles is so huge, so vast, that only a tiny part can be even hinted at in this book; however it will demonstrate conclusively that the entities we have known as Astrology and Numerology are in reality only a tiny facet of what we might call 'The Cycles of Time'.

The book is divided into four major sections — Cycles, Astrology, Numerology, and a summary called 'The Cycles of Time.'

The section on the Cycles themselves shows but the tiniest part of their potential. It demonstrates how all pervading they are, and shows they are like some unseen force guiding us on into the future, like currents in the river of life.

The section on Astrology illustrates the symbolism that has evolved over thousands of years. It offers a discussion on the merits or otherwise of the science, and demonstrates the infrastructure and the antiquities of Astrology. Finally each Sun sign and planet is described individually.

The section on Numerology offers a complete textbook on the subject. It permits an instant, do-it-yourself course in Numerology. The significance of each aspect of the analysis is discussed, as well as the philosophy behind the science. Finally the names and birthdates of over 700 celebrities are listed, for further studies if required.

The last section — 'The Cycles of Time' connects these three factors together. It demonstrates that Astrology and Numerology are but different facets of the entity we call in this book 'The Cycles of Time'. A chapter on the future discusses the course of mankind and the directions we are taking, and the last chapter — 'The Church of Cycles' — demonstrates that there is a direction, there is a purpose, there is meaning to this life.

I hope you enjoy the book.   *John Tatler*

CYCLES

Chapter 1

Cycles — A Phenomenon

The tenor of life
Is cycles of change
What is today
Will not be tomorrow
The aspects now
Will soon re-arrange
So my friend
Wait not on the morrow
For life is a spiral
Ever winding inside
It seems it's repeating
But don't be misled
For the spiral is woven
With patterns untried
The path ever twisting
So watch where you tread.

John Tatler

The Foundation

Thomas Tussner in the sixteenth century wrote: 'It is an ill wind turns none to good.' So it was with the Wall Street stockmarket crash of 1929, for as a result of it a man called Edgar R. Dewey was appointed to investigate the causes for the crash. In his book *Cycles* Mr Dewey recounts how he started on a quest that was to take him a lifetime. Of how in 1940, he was instrumental in setting up The Foundation for the Study of Cycles, and how that body has functioned to the present day.

The Concept of Cycles

What emerges from Mr Dewey's book is an image of something so vast and of such enormity that it is almost incomprehensible. It is a picture showing that everything, or nearly everything, operates in cycles.

We all are aware of night and day, and the four seasons. We associate them with the rotation and orbit of the earth. They dissolve automatically into our day-to-day existence. It is when Mr Dewey confronts us with all manner of other cycles that we become aware that we are living our lives in semi-oblivion by not noticing them.

The pace of modern life is such that we have to have the blinkers on all the time to get the job done, and we tend to develop tunnel vision. Put another way, we see things from the worm's eye view, forgetting the wider vistas of the bird's eye view. We become complacent in our own, snug little niche. We are fogged by our own complacency.

Mr Dewey blows away those fogs of complacency, he confronts us with facts that simply cannot be ignored. He dispels forever any concept that life, as we know it, is random and solely by chance.

The Mechanistic Structure

Mr Dewey paints a picture of a vast, mechanistic, time-based infrastructure that controls or influences everything. He demonstrates that not only do things occur in cycles, but also that those cycles exhibit a common synchronism together. He shows that not only do things operate in a regular sequence of time, but also they are in phase with each other, they share a common trigger point in time, they function as if from the same impulse or cause.

The Sun

Sunspots

Mr Dewey indicates that cycles are not necessarily of a terrestrial origin. On the phenomena of sunspot activity: 'Shortly after World War I a brilliant Russian, Professor A.L. Tchijevsky, published a book with a title guaranteed never to appear on any theatre marquee: *Investigation of the Relationship Between the Sunspot Activity and the Course of the Universal Historical*

Process from the V Century B.C. to the Present Day. Tchijevsky's premise was that disturbances on the Sun — Sunspots — which occur in greater number every eleven years, cause mass excitement here on earth.'

And again: 'In 1878 a British economist, W. Stanley Jevons, advanced a hypothesis that sunspots caused "Commercial Crises". He believed that the variations in the number of sunspots produced variations in crops, and that through this channel cycles in business were triggered. Jevons' work was based in part on the earlier writings of Dr Hyde Clark, who had described an eleven-year cycle in speculation and famine.'

And again: 'In 1881 the English astronomer N.R. Pogson traced an intimate connection between sunspot activity and grain prices in India.'

And again: 'In 1919 Professor Ellsworth Huntingdon advanced the idea that variations in solar radiation had an effect on human beings and thus, in turn, upon business conditions.'

And again: 'In 1939 Loring B. Andrews, a Harvard astronomer, called attention to the apparent correlation over the preceding two hundred years between sunspot activity and wars, international crises, and economic distress.'

And again: 'In 1965 Charles J. Collins, an investment counsellor, published "An Inquiry into the Effect of Sunspot Activity on the Stock Market". In his article he noted that since 1871 the largest stockmarket declines, percentage wise, coincided with or followed years in which average sunspot numbers reached or exceeded a count of fifty.'

Mr Dewey's Foundation for the Study of Cycles has accumulated evidence to connect sunspot activity with many seemingly unrelated things on earth. All the following exhibit synchronism with sunspots on a 5.91 year cycle: combined stock prices, coal stock prices, copper share prices, pig iron prices, railroad stock prices, cotton prices, grouse abundance, copper prices, business failures (inverted).

Solar radiation

Sunspots are the not only evidence of Solar influence. Dr C.G. Abbott of the Smithsonian Institute has spent the greater portion of his life trying to convince people that 'The Solar Constant' is not constant but goes in cycles. The Solar Constant is a measurement, in calories per square centimetres per minute, of the amount of the Sun's energy received.

H.H. Clayton, Chief Forecaster of the Meteorological Service of Argentina, has found correspondence between Solar Radiation and barometric pressure.

Douglas Hunt, in his book *Exploring the Occult* states, 'There is Professor Picardi, Director of the Institute of Physics and Chemistry at Florence, who for some years has been publishing reports on the studies he has been making on the subject of the relations between solar and terrestrial phenomena, and their apparent influence in chemistry, physics and biology.'

The Moon
'He bade the moon come forth;
entrusted night to her;
made her a creature of the dark,
to measure time;
and every month, unfailingly,
adorned her with a crown.'

Enuma elish (2nd Millennium BC)
Mesopotamian creation myth.

Of course, the Sun is not the only astral body that influences us. So does the Moon. The Sun is 26 million times larger in mass than the Moon, but it is 389 times farther away. The Moon therefore exerts an influence on us that is two and a half times greater than that of the Sun.

Tides are the response of the sea to the gravitational forces of both the Sun and the Moon. The gravitational attraction is strongest when it is on a line that passes through the centre of the Earth. Because the Moon exerts the greatest attraction, the tides appear to react to it. Therefore when the waters of the oceans are drawn up, they do so in two bulges, one near to, and one furthest away from the Moon. The two tidal bulges remain in the same position in relation to the Moon, but the rotation of the Earth makes them appear to move round the Earth in 24 hours. As a result a tidal bulge passes the same place on Earth about every 12 hours. These tides are called high water, and the gaps between them are called low water. As the Moon is also moving around the Earth, each high water occurs 12 hours plus an extra 25 minutes later than the previous one.

As the Sun's force is less than that of the Moon so it has less effect on the tides. However, when the Sun, Moon and Earth are roughly in line (at the New or Full Moon) their forces combine to produce spring tides, which are higher than ordinary tides. Conversely, when the Sun and Moon form a right-angle with the Earth (at half Moon), the tides are weak because the Sun's force counteracts that of the Moon. These are lower than ordinary tides and are called neap tides.

The difference in height between high and low water is called the tidal range. At sea this range may be measured in tens of centimetres, but over continental shelves, where the depth of water is less, the range may be up to three metres. Because of their structure, some coasts trap the tides so that much larger ranges result: for example, the Bay of Fundy in Canada has almost 17 metres; St Malo, France, 13 metres. Inland lakes also have tides, but in only the largest ones. Lake Superior, USA, for example, has a tidal range of five centimetres.

The purpose of this lengthy description is to show that it is the combined influence of both Sun and Moon that causes the tides, and their relative positions or phasing that determines the gravitational force exerted.

> 'Oh! Swear not by the moon,
> The inconstant moon,
> That monthly changes in her circle's orb . . .'
>
> *Shakespeare — Romeo and Juliet*

The Lunar Cycle

The Lunar cycle can affect the Earth's weather pattern. Leningrad geophysicist Sergei Timofeyev believes that tidal effects in the Earth's atmosphere influence the circulation of air masses of differing temperatures.

The Lunar cycle is also responsible for temperature fluctuations. With a higher position of the Moon over the horizon, scientists found that cold winters and summers predominate.

It is well known that the time of the full Moon is when our emotions can go a little haywire, and it is an accepted thing in many mental institutions to maintain as full a staff roster as possible over this period. Mental patients are noted for being more violent at the time of the full Moon. The word lunacy came about because of popular belief that the full moon caused madness.

There is definite evidence that the phase of the Moon influences a woman's menstrual period, and also the duration of pregnancy. One major advance in astrology has been the discovery that by studying the position of the Moon at the birth of a woman, her fertile periods may be deduced. Test cases so far have had good results.

And in California the Grunion fish has achieved recognition by being able to select the highest tides for spawning. In some mysterious way the fish are able to select the tides just following the full Moon.

The final word on the effects of the Moon must go to Mr Dewey: 'Dr William F. Petersen was one of the truly great men I have known in my lifetime. Although primarily a medical doctor, he felt that in addition to acquiring greater knowledge about bacteriology and immunology, it was imperative that we do everything possible to relate man to his environment. He believed that however minor they might be, cosmic influences should be taken into account. While studying the Moon's effect on man, Petersen compared various kinds of vital statistics with various phases of the Moon to see if there were any relationships. These statistics included conceptions compared to deaths, the incidence of scarlet fever, the incidence of epileptic attacks, deaths from tuberculosis and others. There appeared to be a definite lunar phase to the chart of deaths from tuberculosis, with an increase of deaths after the full moon. Nevertheless this is only one factor. Certainly, in any individual case, local weather conditions, the condition of the patient, and other related factors are much more important than the phase of the moon. Nevertheless, when put on a lunar axis and smoothed by a three day moving average, the record of deaths does show a high seven days after the full moon and a low seven days before the full moon.'

Human Cycles

In view of all this evidence there can be no doubt that both Sun and Moon exert considerable influence on our lives. Let us now look at some cycles which have a less definitive origin.

Men, it seems, have an emotional cycle that varies with the individual. It can be anything from 16 to 63 days. The average span is about five weeks, the time it takes to move from elation, down to worry, and back up to elation again. Although different individuals have different spans, that period does not generally vary with the person themselves. In other words whatever cycle time they have, they keep to. Women on the other hand have an emotional cycle of some five weeks, that is in addition to the 28-day menstrual cycle. Moreover a doctor in the 1930s discovered that women have a third cycle, of desire, that lasts some 14 days.

Then there are those mysterious Biorhythm cycles that we are now aware of. Discovered at the end of the last century by two German doctors, they have periods of 23 day Physical, 28 day Emotional, and 33 day Intellectual.

Talk to any marriage guidance counsellor and you will find that a seven-year period has great significance with them. Marriages seem to be under most strain at the seventh and fourteenth year junctures, not to mention the famous (or should we say infamous) seven year itch.

Cycles of our Bodies
Our own bodies exhibit their own rhythms and cycles:

The normal heart beats at about 80 beats per minute.
We breathe at the rate of about 22 breaths per minute.
The brain's Alpha rhythms are from 8 to 13 cycles per second.
The brain's Beta rhythms are from 18 to 22 cycles per second.
The brain's Delta rhythms are from 1 to 3 cycles per second.
The brain's Theta rhythms are from 4 to 7 cycles per second.
Our cerebral neurones operate at about 1,000 cycles per second.
The ovaries release an egg every 28 days.
Our kidneys follow a 24-hour cycle.
Our stomach contracts about three times a minute.
We have a muscle cycle of some 12 days duration.
Our red blood cells have a cycle, or life, of some 128 days.
Our bone calcium cycle is some 200 days.

It is no wonder we are affected by cycles, we are but a mass of them ourselves.

The Eight Year Cycles
This concept of cycles becomes the more baffling the further one delves into it. Take the eight-year cycles, listed below, as an example. What possible connection can there be between Red Squirrel abundance and sugar prices, or cotton production, or the growth of pines? It certainly is not the barometric pressure, even if it is on the list. Yet the mystery is that there is a connection. They all operate on the same cycle length, they all peak at the same time, they all turn at the same time.

Whiting abundance
Sweet Potato production
Lynx abundance
Pig Iron prices
Red Squirrel abundance

Steel Ingot production
Butter prices
Sugar prices
Cigarette production
Sales of Goodyear products
Rail Stock prices
Cotton production
Precipitation
Stock prices
Barley for grain
Crude Petroleum production
Coal production
Iron production
Raw Material manufacture
Growth of pines
Barometric pressure
Lead production
Rainfall, USA

Cycles in the Workshop

A good few years ago now, I can remember a technician coming to me and asking my advice about a problem he had. Curious, I followed him back to his bench. Split open in front of him was an electrocardiograph, its innermost secrets on display to the world. Apparently he had been puzzling over a problem that to him simply did not make sense. The fault that he had found was one that was extremely obscure, yet it was the third one that he had seen that week. He could not understand why it was he could go for months, sometimes years, and not see this type of fault occur, and yet in the space of a week he saw three examples.

Together we went through all the possible causes for this mystery, but each time we came up against a blank wall. There seemed to be no rational explanation for the phenomena.

Subsequently, intrigued by this puzzle, I watched the log of repair faults as they were reported each week, and sure enough a pattern did emerge, only a rough indication, but a pattern sure enough. Faults did seem to go in batches, they had a cyclic structure.

Cycle Lengths

These cycles are not all confined to any specific duration. The length of time can vary considerably, and the following list gives only a tiny idea. The point to be realised is that they are all exhibiting this repetitive pattern, and they all seem to be controlled from the same source, whatever and wherever that is. It should also be noted that some of these records go back centuries in time, as is the case with cotton prices (below).

Real Estate activity	18.33 years
Aluminium production	6.4 years
Airplane traffic	5.5 years
General Electric orders received	6.0 years
Immigration, USA	18.2 years
Marriage rates, USA	18.2 years
Death rate, Massachusetts	8.9 years
Taxpayer conscience payments, UK	3.5 years
Corn prices	3.5 years
Cotton prices (1744-1945)	17.25 years

Cycles in nature

Now let us take a look at a table reproduced from Mr Dewey's book, showing 37 examples from the 9.6 year cycle:

Cycles alleged to be 9.6 or 9.7 years in length
In Natural or Social Science Phenomena

Science	Phenomenon	Periods in Years
Mammalogy	Coloured Fox abundance, Canada	9.7
	Coyote abundance, Canada	9 2/3
	Cross Fox abundance, Canada	9.7
	Fisher abundance, Canada	9 2/3
	Lynx abundance, Canada	9.6
	Marten abundance, Canada	9 2/3
	Mink abundance, Canada	9 2/3

	Muskrat abundance, Canada	9.6
	Rabbit abundance, North America	9.6
	Red Fox abundance, Canada	9.7
	Silver Fox abundance, Canada	9.7
	Skunk abundance, Canada	9.7
	Timber Wolf abundance, Canada	9.7
	Wildlife, Canada	9.6
Ichthyology	Salmon catches, Canada	9.6
	Salmon abundance, England	9.6
Ornithology	Goshawk abundance, Canada	9.7
	Grouse abundance, Canada	9.6
	Hawk abundance, Canada	9.6
	Owl abundance, Canada	9.6
	Partridge abundance, Canada/USA	9.6
Entomology	Caterpillar (Tent) abundance, New Jersey	9 2/3
	Chinc Bug abundance, Illinois	9.6
	Tick abundance, Canada	9.6
Dendrochronology	Tree-Ring widths, Arizona	9.6
Agronomy	Wheat acreage, USA	9.6
Climatology	Barometric pressure, Paris	9.7
	Ozone content of atmosphere, London and Paris	9 2/3
	Precipitation, world wide	9.6
	Storm track shifts, North America	9.6
	Magnetic value	9.6
	Hydrology runoff, Rihand & Sone Rivers, India	9 2/3
Medicine	Disease incidence (human heart), New England, USA	9 2/3
	Disease incidence (Tularemia), Canada	9.6
Sociology	War (international battles)	9.6
Economics	Cotton prices, USA	9.65
	Financial crises, Great Britain	9.6

An Analysis of a Cycle

Dr Ravi Batra in his book *The Great Depression of 1990* demonstrates that there is a cycle of depressions that has a 30-year duration. The cycle has not always resulted in a national depression, but in the majority of instances it has. 1990 is the predicted date for the next major depression and Dr Batra demonstrates in detail a similarity of factors existing in the decade prior. He makes a comparison between the economic conditions of the 1920s and those now in the 1980s. Let us review these factors in a six year period of these cycles.

1920
A year of high inflation, high unemployment and high interest rates. A very rare combination.
1980
The same rare combination occurs again.

*

1921
Unemployment rises sharply.
1981
Unemployment rises sharply.

*

1922
Sharp fall in inflation.
Sharp fall in interest rates.
Sharp rise in the stock market.
1982
Sharp fall in inflation.
Sharp fall in interest rates.
A similar rise in the stock market.

*

1923
Banks offer interest on cheque accounts for the first time in history.
Very sharp decline in unemployment.
Stock market continues to rise.
1983
Banks offer interest on cheque accounts for the first time since 1930s.

A decline in unemployment considered the largest in three decades. Stock market continues to rise.

*

1924
Inflation is low, interest rates are stable, and the stock market continues to rise.
1984
The same occurs again.

*

1925
Unemployment falls again.
The stock market rises again, and inflation is unchanged.
A sharp rise in bank failures occurs.
1985
Unemployment falls again.
The stock market rises again, and inflation is unchanged.
A sharp rise in bank failures occurs. 120 banks fail in 1985.

The Connecting Link
The connecting link between these cycles is that they all are the same length, and they all turn at the same time. What agency it is that causes this phenomena is obscure, hidden in fact: by definition, then, occult. Not that the word occult should infer the supernatural, but simply that the answer has not been discovered. It is the presupposition that there is some direct supernatural agency operating which taints the use of the word occult, and overflows by association into the word astrology. I do not believe astrology or numerology operate on any supernatural basis, it is simply that we do not fully know how they work. Before Newton, did people think there was a supernatural influence when apples fell from trees?

Cycles in Religion
Let us now discuss things of a more spiritual nature. Mr Dewey shows that even the variations in church attendance

follow these cyclic laws. Protestant church attendance runs on a nine-yearly interval, which is incidentally nearly directly opposite to the timing of bank deposits, cotton prices, Canadian Pacific ton miles, and other business indicators. To quote Mr Dewey: 'Why is this church-membership rhythm of the same length as one of the main rhythms in economics, but upside down? Why do people join churches in nine-year intervals and why is this rhythm of less strength than before while the rhythm in economics continues with vitality?'

A Library of Cycles

To quote Mr Dewey: 'Every scrap of evidence that we have been able to collect and preserve during the past thirty years can be found in our library at the Foundation. To the best of my knowledge our library contains the most comprehensive collection of cycle material in the world. It is divided into three main sections. In the Data and Research Section we have figures concerning several thousand 'time series'. A series is a string of figures arranged in some order. A time series is a string of figures arranged in order of time. 'Average annual wheat prices in the United States since 1864' is a time series. So is 'Average daily temperature at Boston since January 1, 1967'. Here you can locate data about earthquakes, tree ring thicknesses, geological deposits, rainfall, temperature, barometric pressure, auroras, sunspots, planetary positions, wars, animal abundance, disease, prices, production, crops, transportation, trade, etc.

The second section of the library is where we record the cycle work of others. It contains thousands of articles and clippings and books and reprints of papers in scientific journals alleging cycles of various lengths in the hundreds of phenomena in which such behaviour has been observed.

The third section of our library is perhaps the most interesting. It is concerned basically with interrelationships — and particularly with interrelationships that might throw light on the cause of cycles.'

Cycles — Summing Up

So much of this chapter is owed to the invaluable work and incredible dedication of Mr Dewey. In fact without his work this book would never have been written, maybe never conceived.

In summary I wish to say that it is evident that these cycles do exist, from where or by what agency no one knows. However, they are with us, and if they do not control us, they do influence us. I propose that cycles are the entity we call astrology, and numerology is nothing more than the synthesis of their fundamental rhythms.

One very significant fact that does emerge is that things are apparently not as acausal as we might have supposed. Does this throw more light, or a different light on the work of Carl Jung, and his theory of 'Acausal Synchronicity'?

The earth-shattering aspect of cycles is that with all the destructive nuclear power Man has amassed, we must no longer take a 'Worm's eye view', we must not ignore these forces that could send us to our doom. We must come to terms with these forces, we must try to understand them. The evidence is in our own records. For our very survival we must realise that life is not just a random series of events, it is much more than random chance. Behind the facade of day-to-day life are movements and influences seemingly beyond our control. For our survival, if we cannot sieze the director's baton to the orchestra of our affairs, we must at least know the tune that is playing. Not for nothing does the Bible tell us:

> To everything there is a season,
> And a time to every purpose under the heaven:
> A time to be borne,
> and a time to die;
> A time to plant,
> and a time to pluck up that which is planted;
> A time to kill,
> and a time to heal;
> A time to break down,

and a time to build up;
A time to weep,
and a time to laugh;
A time to mourn,
and a time to dance;
A time to cast away stones,
and a time to gather stones together;
A time to embrace,
and a time to refrain from embracing;
A time to get,
and a time to lose;
A time to keep,
And a time to cast away;
A time to rend,
and a time to sew;
A time to keep silence,
and a time to speak;
A time to love,
and a time to hate;
A time of war,
and a time of peace.

Ecclesiastes 3: (1-8)

ASTROLOGY

Chapter 2

Astrology — a Heritage

A tale begun in other days,
    When summer suns were glowing —
A simple chime, that served to time
    The rhythm of our rowing —

Lewis Carroll

The Origins of Astrology

Astrology today is the culmination of six thousand years of Man's experience. It is claimed that the great library of Nineveh, founded by Assurbanipal, King of Assyria in the seventh century BC, contained astrological manuscripts on clay tablets that dated back to 3800BC. After Assurbanipal's death Nineveh was taken by the Medians and the Chaldean Babylonians. The library was dispersed and the records lost.

The Chaldeans were astute observers and mathematicians. They developed a system of Numerology that is still used by some today. They saw that the changes in the sky went to a pattern, so they drew up the first tables of planetary motions, ephemerides. They prepared their own cosmological system, with twelve constellations, and drew up their own House system, a system very similar to the one in use today; and all of this by the seventh century BC!

As we understand it, the philosophy established at this time was not to change significantly until Kepler in the sixteenth century. Rameses II (13th century BC), Pharaoh of Egypt, fixed the Cardinal signs of Aries, Libra, Cancer and Capricorn.

The Greeks

In about 280BC, Berosus, a priest who had studied extensively in Babylonia, returned to Greece and set up a school for astrology on the island of Cos. Astrology then flourished in Greece, particularly with the Stoics, who had developed their own ideas about celestial forces and destiny. Aristotle said of Berosus, 'He supposes the whole heavens to be a harmonia and a number.'

The horoscope was used to calculate an individual's climacteric years, a particularly critical period in one's lifetime. The word is used in medicine to this day, and in medicine the Greeks built up a complex association between signs and planets with parts of the body. Hippocrates, the father of modern medicine said that a doctor who did not use astrology to aid his diagnosis was more of a fool than a physician.

Ptolemy

Ptolemy (Clausium Ptolomaeus, AD120-180), catalogued over 1,000 separate stars, 300 of them for the first time. He is also credited with the Tetrabiblos, a bible of astrology, that was held in high regard for centuries. It was the most complete manual of the subject yet written. It contained a justification for the belief in planetary influences as well as detailed instructions for interpreting a horoscope.

The Romans

The Roman Empire was equally under the influence of astrology. Emperor Augustus (33BC) had a coin stamped with the symbol of his sign, Capricorn. However, he must have been under other influences as well for he subsequently expelled all astrologers and magicians from Rome.

Roman religion and theories of the afterlife were much influenced by astrology. One of the beliefs current at the time was that when great men died they were transported to the sky, where they lived forever as constellations. Hercules, Perseus, Castor and Pollux were all heroes given this honour.

St Augustine

The early Christian fathers of Rome supported astrology, however St Augustine (AD354-430) declared astrology to be false because it ran contrary to the concept of God's predestined will. Astrology thus entered a period of eclipse that ran well into the Middle Ages.

The Arab World
The Arabs however (Albumasar or Abu Maaschar, AD805-885, in particular), were to keep alive the traditions of classical astrology. Albumasar contributed many works, his *Introductorium in Astronomiam* (Introduction to Astrology), became widely read. It showed the distinct influence of Aristotle.

The Americas
In the New World astrology flourished. The Maya had a Zodiac that consisted of 13 signs, and had priest astrologers who built pyramids to use as observatories. They worked out calendars of planetary movements, one of which was Venus, whose movements were plotted over a period of 384 years.

The Aztecs also had a system of astrology, but the missionary zeal of the Conquistadors swept nearly all evidence away.

The Renaissance
In Europe in the twelfth century astrology was making a comeback. St Albertus Magnus (1200-1280) separated astrology from its pagan associations. A chair of astrology was set up in the University of Bologna and St Thomas of Aquinas (1225-1274) paved the way for better recognition by the church. In 1327 Cecco d'Ascoli, Professor of Astrology at Bologna, was burned at the stake. However, this was because of his heresy not his profession. Regiomontanus (1436-1476), Papal Astrologer, invented a system of astrological house divisions that are still used by some today.

Astrology in the Renaissance period went through a period of popularity and power, due to its acceptance by the church and the encouragement it got from several Popes (Popes Sixtus IV, Julius II, Leo X, Paul III all used astrologers). Queen Elizabeth I of England, presumably influenced by this example,

established John Dee as court astrologer. Denmark, Bohemia
and France all had court astrologers.

Nostradamus

It was in France under Queen Catherine (Catherine de
Medici), that Nostradamus became famous, by predicting the
death of the French King Henri II. Nostradamus was a French
physician, and more a prophet and necromancer than an
astrologer. In one celebrated incident he conjured up a spirit for
45 nights, to show Catherine de Medici the future. She called off
the experiment when the forecasts became decidedly uncomfortable to her.

Copernicus

In 1543 a Polish church official and astronomer called
Nicholas Copernicus, published a book. He gave reasons to
believe that it was the Sun and not the Earth that lay at the centre
of the Solar system. His theory was not new, but it had not been
considered a serious alternative to the belief that it was the Sun
and the planets that revolved around the Earth. The church did
not take to the Copernican idea, in fact they must have taken a
very dim view, for in 1600 they burned Giordano Bruno at the
stake for his persistence with the Copernican theories. Again in
1663, the Inquisition forced Galileo to retract his beliefs about
the structure of the Solar system.

Tycho Brahe

Three years after Copernicus died, Tycho Brahe was
born in Denmark. He was to be an eccentric figure, a Danish
nobleman, and an exponent of the new age of telescopic
astronomy. He did not support the Copernican theories, but
ironically he was to provide the data that would be the proof to
the new ideas. Both astronomer and astrologer, he was to make
some astounding predictions. In 1566 he announced that an
eclipse of the Moon foretold the death of the Sultan of Turkey.
With the King of Denmark's assistance he set up an observatory

on the island of Hven, to draw up an accurate star catalogue. He eventually was appointed Imperial Mathematician to the Holy Roman Empire, and it was here that a German called Kepler was made his chief assistant.

Johannes Kepler

After Tycho Brahe's death in 1601 Kepler was made Imperial Mathematician. Unlike Tycho, he was a follower of Copernicus. So it was he that used Tycho's accurate readings to prove that it was the Earth that revolved around the Sun. This was to be the end of the system developed by Ptolemy in Egypt 1,500 years earlier. Kepler was an astronomer rather than an astrologer, although he stated that there was much value in true astrological thought. He was a disciple of the Pythagorean concept of numbers, and the theory of the vibrations of sound, the harmony that links the distances and dimensions of the universe.

Isaac Newton

In 1687 Isaac Newton published his book *Principia Mathematica*. It opened the doors to the modern phase of astronomy, and brought Kepler's achievements to adulthood. As well as putting forward the theory of gravitation he also made a number of other fundamental advances. He was to be the last of the trio — Copernicus, Kepler and Newton — that many held responsible for the demise of astrology until the middle to late nineteenth century. The paradox was that none of these men were against astrology themselves.

The New Planets

Once Newton's theories took hold the pendulum swung hard toward the rationalist view, and the emphasis was very much on science and astronomy rather than astrology. Sir William Herschell (1738-1822) the German-born, English astronomer discovered Uranus in 1781, and Urbain Le Verrier the French astronomer discovered Neptune in 1846.

The Theosophical Society

It was not until 1875 that astrology took an upturn, with a Madame Blavatsky forming a Theosophical Society. Although not an astrologer, she was interested in the influence of the stars and things occult. This started a new trend of interest in astrology. Astrology in particular gained in popularity under the pen name of Alan Leo, who wrote for the Theosophists before the end of the century.

1875 also marked the birth of a significant figure for astrology — Carl Jung.

Astrology to the Masses

It was not until 1930, in Britain, that a newspaper ran a regular column on astrology. R.H. Naylor began regular contributions to the *Sunday Express* in August 1930.

1930 was also the year that Pluto was discovered.

The Growth of Astrology

Along with the newspaper astrology there has been a corresponding growth in astrology itself. Recent figures in the USA alone indicate more than 15,000 full-time astrologers and over 200,000 part-time astrologers, with the numbers still growing.

The Gauquelins

In 1950 Michel and Francoise Gauquelin started out on a mission to establish astrology. It was a statistical mission that would involve them in research for decades. From the time that Michel Gauquelin published his books detailing his research, astrology began to earn respect from academic quarters. In fact you would find that a considerable number of psychiatrists and psychologists have more than a passing interest in the subject. The Gauquelins have given to astrology the respect it has deserved for centuries.

John Addey

Following hard on the heels of the Gauquelins and actually using the Gauquelin data, John Addey achieved the breakthrough of the ages. For it was he who established a direct connection between astrology and numerology. By using the principles of Fourier analysis he found the rhythms of the cosmic cycles, latent with the astrological birthchart. He established a connection between the birthchart and the Pythagorean concept of numbers.

Chapter 3

Astrology Today

When the Moon is in the Seventh House
And Jupiter aligns with Mars
Then peace will guide the planets
And love will steer the stars.

from *Aquarius*, song in the musical *Hair*.

Astrology — The Study of Man

The study of astrology today means tapping into a storehouse of information about man, about time, and about the heavens. It is unique, a priceless heritage.

Attend a course on astrology today and you learn a new language. You learn about time and how to calculate time, you learn psychology, you learn about Man himself, you learn about life. Astrology is not merely a study of what will happen to people in the course of their lives. It is a study of all human life and all aspects of it. Man's birth, childhood, relationships, self-image, the way others see us, our callings, our drives, our feelings, our energies, they are all there, they are all detailed. In the final analysis the study of astrology is the study of Man, the study of human beings.

The tool of astrology is the horoscope or birthchart. This horoscope chart describes an individual through several systems of symbols. These symbols or categories are the planets, horoscope angles, aspects, houses, and signs. These symbols, systems, categories have evolved and developed over the centuries to what they are today.

Astrology is not just the daily Sun sign columns of newspapers and magazines. Astrology is a science to which its devotees freely, willingly, and wholeheartedly devote their lives. They are thinking people, spiritual people, wise people. They are a group who in the vast majority uphold an integrity that is hard to find in many other areas of human endeavour.

Astrology has developed many connections and affiliations during its journey through the centuries. Astrology in medicine, in psychology, in the arts, in politics — they have all used the science, and astrology has grown because of that use. To quote Jung:

> 'Astrology is assured of recognition from psychology without further restrictions, because astrology represents the summation of all the psychological knowledge of antiquity.'

Astrology and the Sun Sign

Stop anyone in the street and ask them what astrology is. Nine out of ten would say that astrology was predicting the future. That is what astrology means to a majority of people. Why? Because every day in our newspaper or magazine, we look to see what sort of day or week it is going to be. So the trends predicted for the twelve Sun signs have to represent the myriad paths of fate for millions upon millions of people. It is quite understandable that people take the whole thing too literally, and call it ridiculous.

So it is that the very vehicle that daily demonstrates astrology, drags along its own sidecar of misconception and ridicule. The very device that daily promotes astrology, exposes it to its critics; such is this world of the quick and the dead.

The Sun sign owes its fame to R.H. Naylor, who in the 1930s first used it in a column in the British *Sunday Express* newspaper. The idea took hold, adroitly aided by Naylor's predictions, for he proved to be a particularly gifted astrologer. Later in this book are some examples of his prophecies.

So astrology and the Sun sign became the property of the mass media. From that point it never looked back. Its persistence day after day in the tabloids of the world kindled an interest that guarantees its survival.

The serious astrologer may be dismayed about this, but until something else usurps or replaces it, the Sun sign is here to stay. For the Sun sign is by far the most effective way of communicating the complex subject of astrology to the newcomer. It enables him to identify with his sign, to identify with others, and in so doing to identify with astrology itself. The perceived disadvantage with the Sun sign is that it divides humanity into twelve different types. This generalisation that is the Sun sign's advantage, is the factor that the serious astrologer rejects. It is true that you cannot lump everyone together and make out they are the same, yet the Sun sign can be quite accurate in a thumbnail analysis of someone. The question is, how accurate?

Opinions vary, but the general consensus would be that in basic characteristics, the Sun sign is from 60 to 80 percent accurate. Of all the negatives that one can throw at the Sun sign, they somehow fail to counter the mystery, and the delight that understanding others can bring. When you come across an autocratic Leo, it's nice to know that behind that facade is probably a very caring dad. And if you strike a cool, super-efficient Capricorn do you not take to him better when you know that this is his defence? And when you are confronted with the unleashed wrath and fury of an Aries temper, is it not a reassurance to know that soon it will all be gone.

Let's face it: the Sun sign is fun, it's a talking point, a conversation starter. The Sun sign is the introduction agency of the stars. The Sun sign is astrology's calling card.

Astrological Prediction
Astrology has been very successful in predicting the future, but it has also failed dramatically. Why is this so?

I submit it is because astrology is not the device with which to make dramatic predictions. Astrology may predict trends, it can show the way, but it is not the ideal medium to prophesy events. Take World War II as an example; very few astrologers accurately forecast the start. It is as the Viking Runes say: 'Nothing is predestined'.

Certainly the trends are there. Cycles confirm that, as astrology has done for centuries. It is what we do with these trends that makes history. Not cycles, not astrology but our own individual and collective wills.

That is not to say there have not been forecasts that have come true. Accurate forecasts are legion, and here are three that did materialise.

The November issue of *American Astrology* contained the following note: 'The US horoscope . . . shows a progressed Moon-Mars opposition exact at this time, on the heels of which a Moon-Neptune square "matures". In the past such configurations have coincided with personal danger to our head of state, all the more so in view of the grievous attack by Saturn on the President's natal trio of Mars, Mercury and Jupiter, along the Uranus square his Sun (and son, too). November is obviously fraught with perils of several varieties.' President John F. Kennedy was assassinated on November 22nd, 1963.

J.R. Gordon, Editor of the *Sunday Express*, in a foreword to R.H. Naylor's book wrote: 'The first time was in the early hours of that terrible Sunday morning when the R.101 pitched to earth in flames, destroying all but a handful of the crew. I raced by car through the night to the *Sunday Express*, turned the pages of a copy that was wet from the printing presses, and there in the middle of Mr Naylor's weekly article set by some strange freak of Fate, boldly in black type, was a prophesy of the R.101 disaster. The second occasion was equally fantastic. One Saturday afternoon Mr Naylor walked into my office. Lord Castlerosse was sitting at my side, "Can I add something to my article?" said Naylor. "There is going to be an earthquake." "I'm sorry", I said, "but you are too late." Twelve hours later the telephone at my bedside rang, and a voice from the *Sunday Express* office described briefly and vividly to me the earthquake that an hour before had rocked half England.'

I include these particular examples to make an observation. The first was a report rather than a prediction. It discussed the chart in detail and gave a summation. 'November is obviously fraught with perils of several varieties.' The fact that the article appeared in an astrological journal justifies the detailed description of planets and aspects. To the layman such detail is absolutely meaningless. It is pertinent to say that care must be taken to convey proper symbolism. The summation was *responsible* without any other inference.

The other two examples, however, come into the category of prophesy rather than prediction and as a result expose the very structure of astrology to its critics. I cannot perceive how Mr Naylor identified anything other than a dangerous situation from the chart; a specific and exact disaster, I think not. These examples are long in the past, and it is not my intention, or desire, to bring discredit on any individual, living or dead. What I want to draw attention to is the matter of responsible predictions. If someone wishes to make a prophesy, then let them do so without risking discredit to the name of astrology. Let them themselves identify what is prediction and what is prophesy. If they decide it is prophesy, then by all means make it public, if that is their wish. However, do so in their own name, not under the banner of astrology. Let them realise that it was not astrology that communicated the information, it came by another channel. If they have the gift, if they have the power, then by all means use it. First though, identify and know by what means that power came. Let them first know the difference between what is in the chart and what they think is in the chart.

I am reminded of the Roman emperor, Tiberius. He suppressed astrology because he supposed that the predictions could be dangerous to him. However, rather than remain blind to the matter, he secretly consulted astrologers. Frequently, at the end of consultation he would have the astrologer thrown into the sea, to ensure that vital secrets did not leak out. One day an astrologer named Thrasyllus was commanded to appear before the emperor. Duly Thrasyllus presented himself and gave a reading. Afterwards Tiberius asked the astrologer if he ever read his own chart, and if so what did it say. Thrasyllus examined the stars, and became quite disturbed. 'Your majesty', he said, 'my calculations tell me that I am near to death.' Whereupon Tiberius, impressed by this skill, explained that he had intended to have Thrasyllus put to death, but because of this demonstration of expertise had changed his mind. Thrasyllus remained the emperor's astrologer and confidant.

R.H. Naylor in his year book of 1933 wrote: 'Hitler is a son of the elusive planet Neptune. He looks to Mussolini as his example. Whereas Mussolini will go from strength to strength, Hitler will go from weakness to weakness. Finally he and his party will run into a mass of schemes and complications which will eclipse them.' It is fortunate that the harsh penalties of the Roman era are no longer applied.

Twins and Kings

One of the most striking pieces of evidence to support astrology is the fact that those born at the same moment of time and in approximately the same place have personality traits and life patterns that are very similar. Sometimes though this does not occur, and the question is raised — Why not?

It is quite natural to be intimidated by something as inexplicable as this. In fact the astrologer may find himself backed into a corner over the issue. Imagine a serviceman having to explain why a complex piece of electronics broke down. He may have the answer, but if he did not he would be hard-pressed to give a precise account of why the trouble occurred.

Similarly with births that are apparently very similar or identical: why is it that it does not always result in life patterns that are parallel? One reason could be that the birth-time may not have been the same, even a few minutes can make a significant difference to aspects and house placements. However, I feel that the answer lies in our understanding of what astrology is, indeed in our understanding of what life itself is. Imagine if you will, twins born instantly at the same moment of time. Would they be clones, would they be exact duplicates of each other? There have been cases where twins were apparently identical, but even in these cases there were subtle differences. No two people are exactly the same, we are all special, all individual.

We view things on this earth in a very limited way. We only see things from the point of view of what is tangible to us. Therefore those things that we have not had experience of are beyond our realm of understanding. So how can we expect to understand the complexities of creation? It is beyond our experience. The simple fact is that very often similar birth-times and places often result in life patterns that are similar. However these things are not black and white, it is not a hard and fast rule, and who could question it?

Here is my personal analogy to this dilemma. I repeat, my personal view, I do not expect others to accept it. Imagine you are making a jelly. You pour the mixture into a mould, and in time it sets. The mould is the moment in time we are born, it is represented by astrology, by numerology. The time it takes to set is the period on earth we take to form our characters. Some mixtures take longer than others. The mixture? The mixture was made in another time, and another place.

Here are two examples of people with similar birth-times. In the case of George IV and Samuel Hemming there was a close identity of birth conditions. When George IV ascended the throne, Hemming set up in business on his own. When the King married, so did Hemming. Other parallel events took place and finally they both died on the same day. On the day Queen Wilhelmina of the Netherlands married only one other woman in the country was allowed to marry. She was a friend of the Queen, her name was Wilhelmina as well and, yes, she was born on the same day as the Queen.

Chapter 4

The Structure of Astrology

The heavens themselves, the planets and this centre,
Observe degrees, priority, and place,
Insistiture, course, proportion, season, form,
Office, custom, in all line of order,
                                    Shakespeare, *Troilus and Cressida.*

The Elements
The Horoscope is comprised of three key elements: the signs of the Zodiac, the planets and the houses. Everyone will be aware of the signs, often called starsigns, or Sun signs. These are the daily predictions you find in most newspapers. In the chart the signs themselves are relatively inert, it is only when the planets move into them that they begin to exhibit energy, that the signs and planets react together.

The Stage
At this point it would be as well to discuss the solar system. The nature of the solar system as it condensed out of a cloud of gas, was that of a whirling disk of planets. This disk of planets may be likened to the disk around Saturn, the difference being there is nothing like the density of material around the Sun as there is around Saturn. However the analogy is there, and it is that analogy that conceptually connects Saturn to the Sun. In other words, it indicates that Saturn and the Sun are of the same origin. Equally the Milky Way, of which our solar system is part, is a disk of stars revolving around our galaxy.

To return to the disk of planets revolving around the Sun, it is called the ecliptic and is of a relatively narrow proportion. The ecliptic, then, is the stage on which the planets play their part. The backdrop to this stage is a great belt of stars stretching round the earth, 8 degrees wide and 360 degrees in circumference. This is of course the path the Sun appears to trace annually around the earth, it is this that is termed the ecliptic.

An Assumption

Here it is important to point out that the astrologer takes the Earth and not the Sun as the centre of our planetary system. This is quite natural to the astrologer as it is the relative positions of the planets to the Earth that he is interested in. Thus it is not quite so absurd as one might think. The astrologer bases all his calculations and observations on this premise. He assumes that what he has been taught, what has been handed down to him is correct. He assumes that the Earth is the focal point of the planetary forces. He assumes that the planets exert a force or are signifiers of events on the earth, because that is what tradition would have him believe. I believe this not to be the case.

The Ecliptic

To continue, the astrologer pre-supposes that the earth is the centre of the solar system, and to him it makes perfectly good sense to imagine that the other bodies are revolving around him. The ecliptic, then, is the Sun's annual path around the earth. To be more precise if every day you were to mark the point where the Sun's rays struck the earth at a perpendicular you would eventually trace a line we know as the ecliptic.

The Solstices

The ecliptic is always at a slight angle to the equator. It is this angle that causes the seasons to change. If you live in the northern hemisphere then the ecliptic is farthest from the equator on the northern side. The Sun reaches this point at the summer solstice. Similarly, in the depths of winter the Sun is way down at the winter solstice. The opposite applies to the southern hemisphere. The solstices lie on the latitudes known as the tropics of Cancer and Capricorn, because the dates on which they occur coincide with the Sun's position in those signs. The term 'tropic' comes from a Greek word meaning 'turning point'. The point where the ecliptic crosses the equator marks the beginning of spring and autumn, known as the equinoxes.

The Zodiac

To return to the belt of stars we call the Zodiac, if you project the ecliptic into the sky and widen it to 8 degrees you get a strip of constellations through which the Sun revolves. The Sun rises in a different one every month. The Babylonians, who invented the Zodiac, divided it into twelve parts, because there were twelve lunar months in the solar year. Each group of stars was given a name that derived from mythology.

The Precession of the Equinoxes

We should now bring into the matter what is known as the precession of the equinoxes. This means that the annual revolution of the Sun through the constellations is not quite constant. Each spring the position of the Sun in the Zodiac has shifted slightly, so that over a period of two thousand years or so it shifts through an entire sign, thus we talk about the age of Aquarius.

Traditionally the first sign of the Zodiac is Aries, because the Sun rose in Aries at the spring equinox. But since then the equinox has moved into Pisces and is now entering Aquarius. Because of the pre-cession of the equinoxes, the signs of the zodiac, as used by traditional astrologers, no longer coincide with the constellations whose names they bear. For example, an astrologer says that at the spring equinox the Sun rises in Aries, whereas an astronomer would say it rises in Pisces. The astrologer is referring to a purely symbolic constellation tied to a time of year, the astronomer is referring to an actual group of stars.

Two Zodiacs?

So there are two zodiacs. First there is the tropical zodiac whose co-ordinates are the turning points of the solar year, the solstices and the equinoxes. This is the one that traditional astrologers use. Secondly there is the sidereal zodiac which follows the actual positions of the stars in the sky. The co-existence of these two zodiacs is a dilemma for the astrologer.

The Houses

Now to move onto the 'houses'. The houses, like the signs of the zodiac, are twelve in number. However, instead of being divisions in the sky they are divisions of the earth's surface projected into the sky.

The concept of the houses came into being because the early astrologers had the idea that the constellation that was in the sky over the eastern horizon at the time of birth (The Ascendant) must be an important factor in a horoscope. By the same token importance must also be attached to the sign on the meridian (Mid-Heaven), the sign on the western horizon (The Descendant), and the sign immediately below the meridian (Imum Coeli). The areas between these four points were then divided into three sections each, making a total of twelve.

Because the earth makes one complete revolution in 24 hours it follows that the ascendant takes roughly two hours to go through a sign. Hence the necessity to know the exact time of birth of the subject. It has been estimated that without the exact time of birth only 40 percent of a person's horoscope can be determined.

Which House System?

The time that the ascendant stays in a sign is dependent on the latitude of a subject's birth. As a result there are a number of house systems, some taking account of this factor some not. The most popular is the Placidus system named after a Benedictine Monk, Placidus de Titis (1603-1668), who taught mathematics at the University of Padua. It is comment enough on astrology and its hierarchy, that we still use this system after more than 300 years.

The Aspects

When two or more planets are placed together in the same part of the Zodiac, they combine to place a greater emphasis on that area. When two or more planets are within a few degrees of each other they are said to be in conjunction. The closer the two planets are to each other, the more exact is the conjunction and the greater the emphasis. (Imagine two people pulling on a rope; they usually make their presence felt much more than just one person on the rope.) The limit is about 8 or 9 degrees; planets that are farther away than this cannot be said to be in conjunction

Just as two planets together act together, then the angle that separates any two planets will determine whether those planets are in aspect. The following list details the Aspect, the distance, the orb, and the nature.

Aspect	Degrees	Orb	Nature
Conjunction	0	8-9	variable
Semisextile	30	3-4	moderately easy
Semisquare	45	3-4	moderately hard
Sextile	60	6	easy
Square	90	9	hard
Trine	120	9	easy
Sesquiquadrate	135	3-4	moderately hard
Quincunx	150	3-4	moderately hard
Opposition	180	9	hard

Chapter 5

The Academic View

I stood upon that silent hill
And stared into the sky until
My eyes were blind with stars and still
I stared into the sky

Ralph Hodgson

A Difficult Relationship

The accord between astrology and the honoured halls of academia is a difficult relationship. Certainly since the Gauquelins the situation has improved markedly, but there is a long way to go yet. The problem stems from the fact that at best astrology is viewed as a pseudo science, and as such cannot be given any official acknowledgement. The recognition given to astrology by Carl Jung the eminent psychiatrist, has helped the image, but the official view, it seems, remains unmoved.

I have heard of cases where the view of astrology was so intransigent, that astrologers were classed in the same bracket as members of the Flat Earth Society. The various 'Skeptics Societies' seem to mark out astrology as a standard target for regular attacks.

'Objections to Astrology'

The situation was made considerably worse in 1975 when the American magazine *Humanist* persuaded 190 or so leading scientists, including 18 Nobel Prize winners, to sign a statement called 'Objections to Astrology'. In a very correct manner the statement warned the public against the unquestioning acceptance of the predictions given by astrologers, and ended: 'Acceptance of astrology pervades modern society. This can only contribute to the growth of irrationalism and obscurantism. We believe that the time has come to challenge directly and forcefully the pretentious claims of astrological charlatans. It should be apparent that those individuals who continue to have faith in astrology do so in spite of the fact that there is no verified scientific basis for their beliefs and, indeed, that there is strong evidence to the contrary.'

This statement was circulated around the world with the intent that it be published by the newspapers. Later, it came out that a good number of the scientists that signed the statement were not completely familiar with astrology and thus left themselves somewhat open to criticism for condemning something that they did not fully understand.

Whereas one cannot agree with the attitude of those scientists, one has to admit that in light of no tangible evidence their warning was quite proper. Whether it should have been given is another matter. The criticisms given by those scientists identify those aspects of astrology that are perceived by many as needing change.

The Academic View

Carl Sagan.

Notably Carl Sagan, Professor at Cornell University renowned for his television series 'Cosmos', declined from signing the statement. Sending a letter stating that he was unable to endorse the 'Objections to Astrology', he went on to say: 'That we can think of no mechanism for astrology is relevant but unconvincing. No mechanism was known, for example, for continental drift when it was proposed by Wegener. Nevertheless, we see that Wegener was right, and those who objected on the grounds of unavailable mechanism were wrong.'

The Major Factors.

Before full acceptance of astrology can be made by the scientist, it has to be demonstrated that astrology is something that is conceivable, that it can be understood. It is paramount that no vestige of a connection can exist between astrology and any form of magic, but several factors stand in the way of that acceptance.

Firstly, the common attitude, and terminology that would indicate that the planets do influence us. Secondly, the inability to show the mechanism of how astrology works. Thirdly, the understanding and comprehension of the profound significance of the precise moment of birth.

The Astronomer's View

The astronomer Bart. J. Bok writes: 'It seems inconceivable that Mars and the Moon could produce mysterious waves, or vibrations, that could affect our personality in completely different ways. It does not make sense to suppose that the various planets and the Moon, all with rather similar properties, could manage to affect human affairs in totally dissimilar fashions . . . Why should the precise moment of birth be the critical instant in a person's life? Is the instant of conception not basically a more drastic event than the precise moment when the umbilical cord is severed?'

Just a Point of View?

It is significant that a strong supporter of Astrology is a psychiatrist, one who can see the tangible benefits of the science; whereas one of Astrology's major critics is an astronomer, one who finds the science 'inconceivable', who cannot perceive how the planets could exert an influence.

Science and the Scientist

The truth of the matter lies other than in the hard, tangible world of the scientist. Dr H.J. Eysenck in the opening to his book *Uses and Abuses of Psychology* says: 'Clemenceau, in one of his more insightful moments, said that war was too serious a business to be left to the generals. In recent years the feeling has been growing that science is too serious a business to be left to the scientists. From birth to death the life of modern man is conditioned and determined by forces and discoveries which he so little understands that he customarily applies the term "miracles" to them.'

Skepticism and Faith

In the end it all comes back to what you believe: the astrologer has faith in what he does, the scientist is skeptical. Goethe wrote: 'The essential, only and profoundest theme of the history of the world and of mankind, to which all others are subordinate, is the conflict between skepticism and faith.' (notes to *West-Oestlicher Divan*.)

Let the last words be those of Frans Werfel:

> Unto the blind the world is blind;
> Unto the deaf it speaks no word;
> So one will think all faith absurd
> Who in himself no faith can find.

Chapter 6

The Neo Astrologers

If seven maids with seven mops
    Swept it for half a year,
'Do you suppose,' the walrus said,
    'That they could get it clear?'
'I doubt it,' said the carpenter,
    And shed a bitter tear.

Lewis Carroll

The New Rationalists
When Isaac Newton published his work *Principia Mathematica* in 1687 it opened the doors of astronomy to the world, and it slammed shut the door marked 'Astrology' in the mind of man. The reason is self evident. Make something tangible, make it understandable, and you remove the mystery, you strip away the superstition. Astrology then, indeed astrology always, has been perceived as being connected with superstition and black magic.

The New Rationalists of that era claimed astronomy for themselves, and denounced astrology in the process. Thus in 1687 began a long demise for astrology, a demise that was to last nearly 200 years. For it was not until Madame Blavatsky started her Theosophical Society in 1875 that astrology started to emerge from its underworld. It was a slow and gradual ascent until 1930, when the newspapers took hold and astrology became the property of the mass media.

The Newspaper Revolution
In Great Britain R.H. Naylor wrote a column for the *Sunday Express*. Elsewhere in this book are some prophecies of that gifted gentleman. Naylor wrote for the newspapers until the outbreak of World War II in 1939. I only have it on hearsay evidence, but it has been told to me that he only lost his position

then because of an unfavourable prediction. It is said that
Naylor predicted the war would last between five and seven
years. As one might expect this information was not received at
all well, and as a result R.H. Naylor's contributions were ceased
forthwith.

The Gauquelins

Emerging from the war years, astrology was ready and
waiting for its next champion. That person was to come from
France, in 1950, by the name of Michel Gauquelin.

Monsieur Gauquelin and his wife Francoise were to start a
statistical search that would take them two decades. However
before we continue with this story, I should digress a little to lay
to rest a myth that exists about the Gauquelins. It has been said
in astrology circles that Michel Gauquelin started out to
disprove astrology, and in the act of disproving it became a
convert to astrology by his own statistics. That is simply not true.
I would quote here from Michel Gauquelin's book *The Truth
about Astrology*. 'At the age of 20, I was wildly enthusiastic about
everything to do with astrology, although I was equally mad
about painting and tennis. I wanted to do research into
astrology, but had neither the money, nor the time (I was
finishing my studies), nor the application necessary. I did,
however, have a foggy idea of what was involved. I would
go down to the library, between a drawing session in a
Montparnasse attic and a tennis match, and copy out the names
and dates of birth of people who had made a sufficient mark in
life to feature in a dictionary of the famous.'

I make this point because Monsieur Gauquelin's results are
so important to astrology that his attitude when seeking and
sifting his statistics is very relevant to my case. I think that it
would be undisputed to say that in modern times Michel
Gauquelin's contribution to astrology has not been excelled.
The sheer size of his work leaves one agape, whilst his diligence,
patience and determination are equally awesome. From his
book he makes it clear that his sole aim was to provide statistical

evidence for the firm grounding of astrology. As he uncovered evidence, that success fuelled him for his next onslaught. What Gauquelin found was a correspondence of the births of people of differing professions and the diurnal motion of the planets. The diurnal motion of a planet is the time that planet rises and sets in the horoscope chart of an individual.

Let us hear Michel Gauquelin on the subject of the case study of 576 members of the Academie De Medecine: 'Suddenly I was presented with an extraordinary fact. My doctors were not born under the same skies as the common run of humanity. They had chosen to come into the world much more often during roughly the two hours following the rise and culmination of two planets, Mars and Saturn. Moreover, they tended to "avoid" being born following the rise and culmination of the planet Jupiter. After such a long and fruitless search, here I was, confronted with not one but three astonishing results — all from observing the daily motion of planets.'

One has to take one's hat off to Gauquelin for the sheer might of his achievements. He set out to find something and indeed he found it. It reminds one of Edison's words : 'Genius is one percent inspiration and ninety nine percent perspiration.' (Thomas Alva Edison, 1847-1931)

John Addey

There is no doubt that one of the greatest astrologers ever was the late John Addey, an Englishman. Whilst fighting against physical disability, he provided the proof, the connecting link between astrology and numerology. He showed a connection between the astrological cycles produced by the Gauquelins and the Pythagorean theory of numbers. Using Fourier analysis a mathematical technique developed in electronics to measure harmonic distortion. John Addey introduced the concept of the harmonics of the birthchart. Today, every serious student of astrology has to be acquainted with these principles. For Addey demonstrated not just another branch of astrology but a new dimension in which to explore the science of numbers. A new dimension that in reality is at the core of this book, the science of harmonic relationships in the universe. For this book is about harmonics, it is about new dimensions, it is about the harmony of numbers. It is about a fundamental core of truth.

Astrology — a New Look Needed?

Astrology is a very old science. It has collected a mantle, a disguise of vines and creepers through the ages. It is necessary that we cut away those vines and creepers if we are to see what is at its core, at its roots. Gauquelin and Addey have started the pruning, they have shown that it is in the relationship of numbers that the answer may be found.

What is required is a new look at the way we calculate the birthchart. The principles that were developed by Placidus and others are simply outdated. The birthchart, if one wishes to persist with it, should be replaced by a three-dimensional computer-based model. A model in which retrograde planets are forgotten, where the age of Pisces and the age of Aquarius are as of the flat-earth principle. In other words, if you must persist with it then astrology is most overdue for a spring clean.

Chapter 7

The Signs of the Zodiac

The Ram, the Bull, the Heavenly Twins,
And next the Crab the Lion shines,
The Virgin and the Scales,
The Scorpion, Archer, and Sea-Goat,
The Man that bears the Watering-Pot,
The Fish with glittering tails.

Traditional rhyme

The Zodiac

In astrology the ecliptic, or the path taken by the Sun through the heavens, is called the Zodiac. The ecliptic has been divided into 12 parts.

The path taken completes the circle, or 360 degrees, so each division occupies 30 degrees. These twelve divisions are called 'The Signs of the Zodiac' and are named: Aries, Taurus, Gemini, Cancer, Leo, Virgo, Libra, Scorpio, Sagittarius, Capricorn, Aquarius, Pisces.

The belt of stars, or constellations, contained within the eight degrees of the ecliptic represents a pictorial history of the evolution of the universe. It has come to be a synthetic diagram of human progress through the ages.

Each of the twelve divisions, then, has its own constellation of stars, and symbolises an aspect of man.

The twelve signs are understood from many different points of view, just as man is understood from differing perspectives. This understanding, or these perspectives, can be termed classifications. Below are listed these classifications of the signs of the zodiac.

The Elements

The four elements are: Fire, Earth, Air, Water. They correspond to: Spirit, Body, Mind, Soul.

They are distributed in the signs:

Fire (Spirit)	— Aries, Leo, Sagittarius
Earth (Body)	— Taurus, Virgo, Capricorn
Air (Mind)	— Gemini, Libra, Aquarius
Water (Soul)	— Cancer, Scorpio, Pisces

The Constitutions

The signs have a constitutional nature that is divided into three categories:

Cardinal	— active and forceful
Fixed	— determined and masterful
Mutable	— passive and servile

They are distributed in the signs:

Cardinal	— Aries, Cancer, Libra, Capricorn
Fixed	— Taurus, Leo, Scorpio, Aquarius
Mutable	— Gemini, Virgo, Sagittarius, Pisces

The Polarities

Positive — Aries, Gemini, Leo, Libra, Sagittarius, Aquarius
Negative — Taurus, Cancer, Virgo, Scorpio, Capricorn, Pisces

The Sex of the Signs

Masculine — Aries, Gemini, Leo, Libra, Sagittarius, Aquarius
Feminine — Taurus, Cancer, Virgo, Scorpio, Capricorn, Pisces

The Human Signs

The human signs are Gemini, Virgo, Aquarius

The Bestial Signs

The bestial signs are Aries, Taurus, Leo, Capricorn

The Violent Signs

The violent signs are Aries, Gemini, Scorpio, Capricorn

The Bicorporeal Signs

The double signs are Gemini, Sagittarius, Pisces

The Fruitful Signs
The fruitful signs are Taurus, Cancer, Scorpio, Sagittarius, Pisces

The Sterile Signs
The sterile signs are Aries, Gemini, Leo, Virgo

The Mute Signs
The mute signs are Cancer, Scorpio, Pisces

The Voice Signs
The voice signs are Gemini, Libra, Aquarius

*

The Signs

The following pages give brief descriptions of the individual signs of the zodiac; however, when reading the signs refer also to the descriptions of the Ruling Planets to view a perspective of the motive forces and symbology behind the signs.

ARIES

Key Words — I am
March 21 — April 20   Symbol — The Ram
Ruling Planet — Mars   Ruling Number — 9 (Positive)
Positive — Fire — Cardinal — Masculine — Bestial — Violent
— Sterile

The myth
Phrixus falsely condemned to death was rescued by a golden Ram. He reached safety and sacrificed the Ram to Zeus, who placed the Ram's likeness in the heavens.

Biblical association

New Testament — Mark : Archangel — Malchidial : Angel —
Shariel : Apostle — Matthias : Tribe — Gad

Characteristics

The first sign of the zodiac, forceful and self assertive, with drive
and initiative. Often has natural qualities of leadership. Single-
mindedness of purpose can verge on ruthlessness, and he can
make himself unpopular with others. Fierce tempered, passionate in love and strong in sexual feelings. Is generally open
and direct and completely honest with himself. Such lack of
guile can be interpreted by others as being thoughtless and
tactless. Extremely demanding, can be possessive in love, and
paradoxically very sensitive himself.

Career

Surgeon, butcher, psychologist, psychiatrist, foundry worker,
explorer, engine driver, trade unionist, dentist, sportsman.

Anatomical affinity

Skull and face: the muscles used in eating, talking, smiling, etc.
The temporal and internal carotid arteries : the Cephalic
veins.

Famous Aries people

Gloria Swanson, Bette Davis, Joan Crawford, Houdini, Vincent
Van Gogh, Lenin, Sir Joseph Lister, Swinburne, Thomas
Jefferson, Charlie Chaplin, Adolf Hitler, Peter Ustinov.

Regions of the World

England, Denmark, Germany, Burgundy, Palestine, Syria,
Japan

TAURUS

Key Words — I have
April 21 — May 21   Symbol — The Bull
Ruling Planet — Venus   Ruling Number — 6 (Positive)
Negative — Earth — Fixed — Bestial — Fruitful

The myth

Zeus, disguised as Taurus the white bull, courted Europa whilst he bore her on his back. When Zeus changed back to his normal form he placed Taurus in the heavens.

Biblical Association

Prophet — Harrai : Archangel — Asmodeus : Angel — Araziel Tribe — Ephraim : Disciple — Thaddeus

Characteristics

A down-to-earth, practical individual to whom work is no stranger, in fact he can delight in it. Generally a strong physique hides a warm, friendly, loving nature. However when enraged he can literally become the bull that is his symbol. Others may mistakenly accuse him of being boring or pedantic. This sign represents the realisation of true material values. In love, prefers a partner who will give a calm home life.

Career

Horticulturist, businessman, farmer, architect, sculptor, singer, surveyor, jeweller, civil servant, accountant, auctioneer, civil servant, banker, art dealer.

Anatomical affinity

The neck, throat, ears, pharynx, eustachian tubes, tonsils, upper esophagus, palate, thyroid gland, vocal chords. Muscles in the front and back of the neck. The carotid and basilar arteries and the jugular vein.

Famous Taurus people
Pierre Curie, Pope John Paul II, Karl Marx, Bing Crosby, Sigmund Freud, Ella Fitzgerald, Queen Elizabeth II, Dame Margot Fonteyn, Orson Welles.

Regions of the World
Ireland, Poland, Asia Minor, Georgia, Caucasus, Grecian Archipelago, Cyprus, White Russia.

GEMINI

Key Words — I Think

May 22 — June 21	Symbol — The Twins
Ruling Planet — Mercury	Ruling Number — 5 (Positive)

Positive — Air — Mutable — Masculine — Human — Violent — Bicorporeal — Sterile

Origin
Egyptian — 'The Two Stars'

Biblical association
Gemini is biblically referred to as Cain and Abel, and as Simeon and Levi : Archangel — Ambriel : Angel — Sarayel : Prophet — Zachariah: Disciple — Simeon : Tribe — Manasseh

Characteristics
A typical Gemini is quick-witted, resourceful, and can turn his hand to many activities. However he may find it difficult to stay at anything for a long time. He can fall into the trap of being jack-of-all-trades and master of none. Gemini people love to talk and make entertaining companions. They also excel in writing or any art that requires communications. They can sometimes have the urge to lead a double life, moving easily from one role to another. In love a Gemini can be playful and flippant.

Career
Journalist, actor, broadcaster, commentator, lecturer, writer, linguist, secretary, travel agent, chauffeur, salesman, navigator, postman.

Anatomical affinity
Gemini rules the nervous system. The upper ribs, collarbones, shoulder blades, and bones in the upper arms, forearms, wrists and hands. The veins and arteries associated with the arms, shoulders, rib cage and lungs.

Famous Gemini people
John F. Kennedy, Queen Victoria, Prince Aly Khan, Sir Laurence Olivier, Charles II, Catherine the Great, Jane Russell, Judy Garland, Bob Dylan, John Wayne.

Regions of the world
United States of America, Belgium, Brabant, Lombardy, Lower Egypt, Sardinia, Armenia, Tripoli, Flanders, Wales and West of England.

CANCER

Key Words — I Feel

June 22 — July 22   Symbol — The Crab
Ruling Planet — Moon   **Ruling Number — 2**
Negative — Water — Cardinal — Feminine — Fruitful — Mute

Origin
Babylonian — The Crab : Egyptian — Two Turtles (Stars of the Water)

Biblical association
In the Gospel, Issachar is likened to a strong ass which at one time was the symbol of cancer. Tribe — Issachar : Archangel — Muriel : Angel — Pakiel : Prophet — Amos : Disciple — John

Characteristics
Tender-hearted, sometimes touchy and extremely sensitive, the crabs show a hard exterior, but very soft inside. They wish to identify with the home, yet seem to be reluctant to settle down. They fear the consequences of their vulnerability and are apt to be extremely self-protective as a result. Their sensitivity does cause problems when matters of the heart are involved. The path of true love, etc.

Career
Businessman, nurse, caterer, hotelier, fisherman, boat builder, housewife, sailor, children's nurse, kindergarten teacher, historian, curator, antique dealer.

Anatomical affinity
Breasts, chest, stomach, pancreas. The breast bone and lower ribs. The intercostal muscles. The diaphragmatic arteries (those serving the stomach). The mammary, gastro-epiploic and diaphragmatic veins.

Famous Cancer people
Julius Caesar, Duke of Windsor, Dr Alfred Kinsey, Gina Lollobrigida, John Glenn, Ginger Rogers, Louis Armstrong, Yul Brynner.

Regions of the world
Scotland, Holland, Zeeland, North and West Africa, Mauritius, Paraguay, Tunis, Algiers.

LEO

Key Words — I Will
July 23 — August 23   Symbol — The Lion
Ruling Planet — The Sun   Ruling Number — 1
Positive — Fire — Fixed — Masculine — Bestial — Sterile

The myth

The Nemean lion had a pelt that was proof against iron, bronze and stone. Hercules fought the lion and killed it, but not before losing a finger in the battle. The constellation marks the lion's bravery.

Biblical association

Leo the lion is one of the beasts of the cherubim. Jacob assigned this sign to the tribe of Judah. Apostle — Peter : Archangel — Verchiel : Angel — Sharatiel : Prophet — Hosea

Characteristics

A person born with his Sun in Leo is almost invariably a strong personality with a taste for leadership. The sign has a traditional association with monarchs and rulers. At his best a Leo is a thoroughly likeable person, warm and outgoing, with a great capacity to attract the friendship, loyalty, and respect of others. On the negative side his traits are vanity, pomposity and a certain lust for power.

Career

Actor, dancer, teacher, youth worker, manager, director, sportsman, commissionaire, jeweller.

Anatomical affinity

The heart, spinal marrow, nerves and fibre. The dorsal vertebrae. The muscles of the back and shoulder. The aorta, anterior and posterior coronary and the coronary veins.

Famous Leo people

Dr Albert Sabin, Orville Wright, Benito Mussolini, Fidel Castro, Menachem Begin, Mae West, Shelley, Alfred Hitchcock, Mick Jagger, Neil Armstrong.

Regions of the world

France, Italy, Bohemia, Sicily, Chaldea to Bassorah, Roumania, Apulia, The Alps

VIRGO

Key Words — I analyse
August 24 — September 23   Symbol — The Virgin
Ruling Planet — Mercury   Ruling Number — 5 (Negative)
Negative — Earth — Mutable — Feminine — Human —
Sterile

The myth

Virgo was the daughter of Jupiter and Themsis and was goddess of justice. When the Golden Age ended and men defied her rule she returned to the heavens in disgust.

Biblical association

Virgo bearing the 'Sheaf' was called 'The House of Corn' or Bethlehem and is sometimes related to Joseph. Tribe — Nephtali : Archangel — Hamaliel : Angel — Shelathiel : Discipline — Andrew.

Characteristics

The person born with their Sun in Virgo is cool, practical, discriminating and often critical. They are often modest and retiring, but faithful and intellectual. They have a good memory, reasoning power and are fond of the arts, reading and collecting. Concerned with matters of health, they are advocates of physical fitness and a good diet. They often tend to try and live by impossible standards.

Career

Secretary, analytical chemist, scientist, statistician, gardener, accountant, teacher, inspector, craftsman.

Anatomical affinity

The bowels or the abdomen, the duodenum and peritoneum. The rectal and abdominal muscles. The arteries serving the digestive system, the intestinal veins.

Famous Virgo people
Tolstoy, Goethe, Lyndon Johnson, Peter Sellers, Queen Elizabeth I, Maurice Chevalier, Greta Garbo, Rocky Marciano, Sean Connery.

Regions of the world
Turkey, Switzerland, West Indies, Assyria, Mesopotamia, Crete, Croatia, Silesia, Babylonia, Thessaly, Kurdestan, Greece, Virginia, Brazil.

LIBRA

Key Words — I Balance

September 24 — October 23   Symbol — The Scales
Ruling Planet — Venus   Ruling Number 6 (Negative)
Positive — Air — Cardinal — Masculine — Voice

Origin
In Babylonian religions the constellation of Libra was associated with the judgement of the living and the dead. In Zibanitu the scales weighed souls. In Egypt the harvest was weighed when the Moon was full in Libra.

Biblical associations
Archangel — Zuriel : Angel — Chedquiel : Disciple — Bartholomew : Apostle — Luke : Tribe — Asher

Characteristics
A person born with their Sun in Libra needs harmony and balance, avoiding conflict if at all possible. If Libras are involved in a dispute they will go out of their way to bring about a compromise. They are warm and good companions. They have a natural elegance that enables them to move through life with some ease. Laziness can be a failing as are fluctuating moods. The inability to come to a rapid decision is a classic trait, they must weigh everything up first.

Career
Dress designer, milliner, anything to do with clothing industry, diplomat, beautician, welfare worker, receptionist, valuer, high wire performer, any work associated with art.

Anatomical affinity
The lumbar region in general, the kidneys, loins, ovaries. The lumbar vertebrae just below the ribs. The muscles of the lower back and the top of the pelvic bone. The arteries and veins associated with the kidneys. Libra represents equipoise, distillation, sublimation and filtration.

Famous Libra people
Mahatma Ghandi, Horatio Nelson, D. Eisenhower, Carol Lombard, Al Martino, Pope Paul VI, Graham Greene, Shirley Temple, Oscar Wilde, Julie Andrews.

Regions of the world
Algeria, Barbary, Bavaria, China, Judea, Jutland, Morocco, Norway, North Syria, Transvaal, Catalonia, Queensland.

SCORPIO

Key Words — I Desire
October 24 — November 22   Symbol — The Scorpion
Ruling Planets — Pluto and Mars
Ruling Number — 9 (Negative)
Negative — Water — Fixed — Feminine — Violent — Fruitful — Mute

The myth
At Juno's command the Scorpion rose to attack Orion. The Scorpion also caused the horses of the Sun to bolt when driven by the boy Phaethon. Jove attacked it with a thunderbolt.

Biblical association
Archangel — Barkiel : Angel — Saitziel : Tribe — Dan : Disciples — Judas Iscariot and Philip

Characteristics
A person born with their Sun in Scorpio is temperamental, aggressive and ambitious. They possess great powers of leadership but tend to command obedience by fear rather than affection and respect. They can be extremely secretive, and do not divulge information unless they need to or it suits them. They have deep layers of complexity in their make-up, with strong sexual overtones. Scorpios can be very unforgiving.

Career
Psychiatrist, psychologist, detective, policeman, butcher, undertaker, pathologist, sewage worker, pharmacist, psychic, spiritualist, criminal, insurance, armed forces.

Anatomical affinity
Scorpio is associated with the reproductive organs, the bladder, ureters, pelvis, of the kidney, urethra, prostate gland, groin, rectum, colon, nostrils and sense of smell.

Famous Scorpio people
General De Gaulle, Richard Burton, Martin Luther, Rommel, Picasso, Katherine Hepburn, Billy Graham, Petula Clark, Indira Ghandi, Prince Charles.

Regions of the world
Austria, Indo-China, Tibet, Caspian, Upper Egypt, Savoy, North China, Burma, Argentina.

SAGITTARIUS

Key Words — I See
November 23 — December 21   Symbol — The Hunter
Ruling Planet — Jupiter   Ruling Number — 3 (Positive)
Positive — Fire — Mutable — Masculine — Bicorporeal — Fruitful

The myth
With his two faces, animal and human, Sagittarius was the centaur Cheiron who raised Jason, Achilles and Aeneas. He was the son of Philyra by Cronus and the father of Zeus who, surprised in the act, turned himself into a stallion and galloped off, leaving Philyra. So disgusted at her half human, half horse infant, Philyra turned herself into a linden tree.

Biblical association
Archangel — Adnachiel : Angel — Samequiel : Prophet — Zephaniah : Apostle — James son of Zebedee : Tribe — Benjamin

Characteristics
A person born with their Sun in Sagittarius is outgoing, cheerful and jovial. They have intellect and a capacity for deep thought. Both physically and mentally restless, they can be quick tempered with strong passions. They are renowned for their love of sport and the outdoors. An independent nature makes it hard for them to be subservient or even to make partnerships on an equal basis. They love freedom, can be self-assertive and are often quite boisterous.

Career
Teacher, professor, lecturer, philosopher, lawyer, barrister, interpreter, horse trainer, veterinary surgeon, explorer, travel agent, sportsman, jockey, priest, writer, publisher, librarian, bookseller, theologian.

Anatomical affinity
The sacrum, the sciatic nerve, the hips and thighs. The sacrum and tibia bones, the muscles of the thighs and buttocks. The arteries and veins serving the thighs and buttocks.

Famous Sagittarius people
Winston Churchill, Beethoven, Berlioz, Disraeli, Walt Disney, Boris Karloff, Jane Fonda, Frank Sinatra, Noel Coward, Maria Callas.

Regions of the world
Australia, Arabia, Cape Finisterre, Dalmatia, Hungary, Moravia, Sclanovia, Spain, Tuscany, Provence, Madagascar.

CAPRICORN

Key Words — I Use
December 22 — January 20   Symbol — The Goat
Ruling Planet — Saturn   Ruling Number — 8 (Positive)
Negative — Earth — Cardinal — Feminine — Bestial — Violent

Origin
The ancient Babylonian god was Ea, 'The Antelope of the Subterranean Ocean'. The fish-tailed goat called 'Kusarikku', the Fish-ram. There are also references to Pan, whose mother, repelled by his ugliness, ran from him. Pan's prowess in seducing nymphs was legendary.

Biblical association
Archangel — Hanael : Angel — Saritiel : Prophet — Nathum : Disciples — Simon, Peter and Thomas : Tribe — Zebulon.

Characteristics
A person born with their Sun in Capricorn will exude an air of reserve in their demeanour. Often apparently very respectable, their position in life is of great importance to them. They are

capable of extremely hard work and sometimes may be considered a plodder. Often they will display a cryptic but bright sense of humour. They can be relied upon to honour their commitments. Their sense of security is vital to them, thus they view tangible material assets of great importance. They achieve their goals by a dogged persistence towards their objective.

Career
Civil servant, mathematician, politician, scientist, osteopath, engineer, farmer, mineralogist, architect, musician, builder, surveyor, dentist, manager, administrator, accountant, banker.

Anatomical affinity
The knee, patella bone, the muscles of the knee. The veins and arteries of the knees.

Famous Capricorn people
Gladstone, Loretta Young, Jane Wyman, Mao Tse Tung, Elvis Presley, Richard Nixon, Sir Isaac Newton, Muhammad Ali, Marlene Dietrich.

Regions of the world
India, Punjab, Afghanistan, Thrace, Macedonia, Illyria, Albania, Bosnia, Bulgaria, Saxony, Mexico, Lithuania, Orkney Islands.

AQUARIUS

Key Words — I Know
January 21 — February 19   Symbol — The Water Carrier
Ruling Planets — Saturn and Uranus
Ruling Numbers — 4 and 8 (Negative)
Positive — Air — Fixed — Masculine — Human — Voice

Origin

There would seem to be no strong myths associated with Aquarius. However, the god Hapi watering from two jars was an ancient symbol of the River Nile. The goddess GU.LA, the Babylonian equivalent of Aquarius was the patron of childbirth and healing.

Biblical association

Aquarius is associated with John the Baptist and it corresponds to Jacob's son, Reuben. Archangel — Cambiel : Angel — Tzakmiqiel : Prophet — Habukkuk : Disciple — Matthew : Tribe — Reuben

Characteristics

A person born with their Sun in Aquarius is a logical-thinking individual with strong humanitarian instincts. They find it easier to love humanity as a whole than to establish a deep relationship with one person. An advocate of change, sometimes impatient for it, they are interested in science, logical thinking and rationality. They can be impatient of traditional restraints and can have an unwitting desire to test the love and affection that others have for them. Often they alienate themselves rather than face an emotional issue.

Career

Scientist, writer, sociologist, charity worker, astronomer, astrologer, archaeologist, industrial worker, electronics engineer, radiographer, meteorologist, Air Force, airlines, computer engineer, programmer, humanitarian.

Anatomical affinity

The coccyx at the base of the spine, the calves and ankles. The lower leg bones and shins. The veins and arteries serving the lower leg.

Famous Aquarius people
Charles Dickens, Cesar Romero, President Ronald Reagan, Yehudi Menuhin, Franklin Roosevelt, Abraham Lincoln, Clark Gable, Jack Lemmon, Lord Byron.

Regions of the world
Arabia, Prussia, Russia, USSR, Poland, Sweden, Tartary, Westphalia, Abyssinia.

PISCES

Key Words — I Believe
February 20 — March 20   Symbol — The Fishes
Ruling Planets — Jupiter and Neptune
Ruling Numbers — 7 and 3 (Negative)
Negative — Water — Mutable — Feminine — Bicorporeal — Fruitful — Mute

The myth
Venus and Cupid frightened by the giant Typhon threw themselves into the Euphrates and became fishes. Minerva, to mark the event, placed the fishes in the heavens.

Biblical association
Archangel — Amnitziel : Angel — Barchiel : Prophet — Joel : Tribe — Simeon, Ephraim.

Characteristics
A person born with the Sun in Pisces tends to be both sensitive and intelligent. They would avoid confrontation and can be rather passive or negative in their attitude. They may often drift off into their own private world of dreams and fantasy. Alcohol and drugs can present themselves as hazards at times. They do have the tendency, sometimes, to swim both ways in life, and at the same time too.

Career
Actor, dancer, writer, poet, anything to do with shoes, Navy, seaman, nurse, medical profession, hypnotist, illusionist, magician, priest, nun, photographer.

Anatomical affinity
The feet and toes, especially the soles. The bones of the feet and toes. The muscles that control the feet and toes.

Famous Pisces people
Chopin, Einstein, Harold Wilson, Jennifer Jones, Elizabeth Taylor, Rudolph Nureyev, Edward Kennedy, Michelangelo, Robert Conrad, Samuel Pepys.

Regions of the world
Portugal, Calabria, Galicia, Normandy, Nubia, Sahara Desert.

Chapter 8

The Planets

Soon as the evening shades prevail,
The Moon takes up the wondrous tale,
And nightly to the listening Earth
Repeats the story of her birth.

Whilst all the stars that round her burn,
And all the planets in their turn,
Confirm the tidings as they roll,
And spread the truth from pole to pole.

Joseph Addison

The Solar System
The star we call the Sun is just one of approximately 100,000 Suns forming a spiral-shaped galaxy which we call the Milky Way. The Sun is relatively insignificant in the galaxial scheme of things, larger and brighter than some but much smaller and dimmer than many other stars.

The Milky Way is but one of some two dozen local galaxies. Beyond them are millions of other galaxies.

Around our Sun rotate at least nine other planets. Their orbits are not circles but ellipses, and all are in roughly the same plane.

The Planetary System
There is an order and uniformity in the solar system. The physical order of the planets is fairly regular.

All of the planets move counter-clockwise around the Sun. All of the Moons move counter-clockwise around their respective planets. All of the planets line up in nearly the same plane in space, except for Pluto which tends to be eccentric. Every orbit of the planets is elliptical. The farther a planet is from the Sun, the slower it travels.

The Influence of the Planets

Since ancient times each planet has been given a special relationship with a sign of the zodiac. This pattern of rulership was augmented by the discovery of Uranus in 1781, Neptune in 1846 and Pluto in 1930. The symbolism of the planets is vital to Man's awareness of himself. Carl Jung said: 'As we know, science began with the stars, and mankind discovered in them the dominants of the unconscious, the "gods", as well as the curious psychological qualities of the Zodiac: a complete projected theory of human character.' (*Jung, Psychology and Alchemy*)

The Nature of the Planets

The benefic planets are Jupiter and Venus. Jupiter is known as 'The Greater Benefic', Venus as 'The Lesser Benefic'. Mars, Saturn and Uranus are known as the malefics.

Mercury, Neptune and Pluto are neutral planets. Their influence is good when well aspected, and malefic when adversely aspected.

Planetary Rulership

Certain planets and signs are closely related, both in manner and in influence. Thus the planet is said to rule the sign in which it best expresses its natural qualities. This harmonious relationship signifies that a sign is the 'home' or 'domicile' of the planet.

Planetary Detriment

A planet is said to be in its detriment when it is located in the sign opposite that which it rules.

Planetary Exaltation

A sign can be said to traditionally make a planet 'exalted'. The Sun is exalted in Aries, and the Moon is exalted in Taurus. However, if a planet is located in the sign opposite to that in which it is exalted then it is said to be in its 'fall'. Thus the

Sun is in its fall in Libra, and the Moon is in its fall in Scorpio.

Planetary Dignities and Debilities

The positive and negative aspects of a planet's influence are expressed as its 'Dignity' or 'Debility'. The dignity or debility may also express its influence. Thus in Aries Mars expresses its dignity or positive aspects, and in Libra Mars expresses its debility or negative side.

Planetary Angularity

A planet can be said to be angular when it falls within eight degrees of the Ascendant, Descendant, MC or IC. This position strengthens the planet's effect on a subject.

Mutual Reception

A planet is in 'Mutual Reception' with another planet when each falls in the sign ruled by the other: for instance, when Mercury is in Libra (ruled by Venus) and Venus is in Virgo (ruled by Mercury). Two planets in mutual reception are said to work together for the subject's benefit, each strengthening the effect of the other.

The Planets

The following pages detail each planet individually, giving astronomical data, symbolism, dignities and detriments.

THE SUN

Key Words — Power, Vitality

Physical data
Mean diameter : 1,392,000 km
Equatorial rotation speed : 25.4 days
Inclination of equator to ecliptic : 7.15
Mean density (water = 1) : 1.4

Mass to energy conversion rate : 4,000,000 tonnes/second
Temperature at centre : 14,000,000°C
Temperature at surface : 5,500°C
Mean Distance from Earth : 149,600,000 km

Mythology
There have been many Sun gods throughout the world.
In Western Europe the main one was Apollo, son of Zeus and
Leto, born on Mount Cynthus. He was the conception of a
golden son, beautiful, just and a benefactor. He was always
depicted as an extremely handsome young man, lithe, vigorous,
beardless, with thick, long hair. Clad in a simple robe, or naked,
he ruled the seasons and was the god of agriculture.

Astrological data
Rules Leo
Exalted in Aries
Detriment — Libra
Fall — Aquarius

Associations
The Sun represents character, willpower, power, vitality,
leadership and creativity. It signifies hope, courage, honour,
glory, the urge to achieve, magnanimity and the aspirations of a
person. The Sun is hot, dry, electric, masculine and inflam-
matory. The Sun governs the sides, the back, the spine and the
heart. Its action is to illuminate, vitalise, individualise and
stabilise. It associates with heads of state, fatherhood, royalty,
creativity and games.

Keywords

Positive (Dignified)
Creative, generous, big-hearted, joie-de-vivre, organisational
ability, love of children, affectionate, magnanimous, ambitious,
honourable, lofty, dignified, loyal, faithful, distinguished,
gallant.

Negative (Debilitated)
Pompous, arrogant, domineering, gushing, proud, extravagant, condescending, overbearing, bombastic, disdainful, despotic, arrogant, authoritative, haughty.

THE MOON

Key Words — Response, Instinct

Physical data
Mean diameter : 3,476 km
Rotation speed : 27.3 days
Sidereal period : 27.3 days
Inclination of equator to ecliptic : 5.15
Inclination of equator to orbit : 6.73
Mean density (water = 1) : 3.34
Day surface temperature : 110°C
Night surface temperature : -173°C
Mean distance from earth : 384,000 km

Mythology
Hecate, a Moon goddess, brought riches and wisdom to men. Circe, another Moon goddess, was less benevolent and brought upon Man evil spells and enchantments; whilst Selene bathed each night in the ocean and then rode her chariot across the sky.

Astrological data
Rules Cancer
Exalted in Taurus
Detriment — Capricorn
Fall — Scorpio

Associations
The Moon represents instinct, habit, the personality, feeling, emotion, memory, imagination, receptivity, impressionability.

The desire for new experience, domestic environment, cherishing and protective impulses. It signifies women in general. It is associated with birth and motherhood, the digestive system, stomach and breasts. The sympathetic nervous system, body fluids, nutrition, emotional disturbance and personal habits, the home, family and ancestors.

Keywords

Positive (Dignified)
Passive, patient, tenacious, imaginative, sensitive, a material nature, sympathetic, receptive, good memory, reflective, pliable, variable, refined, domestic, public, maternal, productive, adaptable.
Negative (Debilitated)
Moody, clannish, changeable, unreliable, gullible, narrow-minded, reluctance to forgive, frivolous, weak, conceited, common, nonsensical, personal, childish, luny.

MERCURY

Key Word — Communication

Physical data
Mean diameter : 4,880 km
Rotation speed : 58.7 days
Sidereal period : 88 days
Inclination to orbit : 0 Degrees
Mean density (water =1) : 5.4
Day surface temperature : 427°C
Night surface temperature : -173°C
Mean distance from sun : 50,000,000 km

Mythology
Mercury first appeared in Roman mythology about the fifth Century BC. Eventually associated with the Greek god Hermes. Hermes/Mercury was the god of travellers and was associated

with trade and commerce. He also conducted souls of the dead to the underword. The messenger of Zeus, he was witty and quick talking, often dashing to and fro between earth and heaven, usually naked with winged heels and hat. He always carried a staff entwined with serpents.

Astrological data
Rules Gemini and Virgo
Exalted in Virgo
Detriment — Sagittarius
Fall — Pisces

Associations
Mercury represents the power of communication, inter-pretation, self expression, intelligence, reason and mobility. It is associated with the brain, reason, intellect, the co-ordination of the nervous system, the respiratory system, mental perception and the thyroid gland. It signifies day-to-day travel, your car, motor scooter, bicycle, etc.

Keywords

Positive (Dignified)
Perceptive, observant, intellectual, discriminating, accomplished, clever, skilful, vigilant, adroit, fluent, lucid, expeditious, studious, concentrative, the urge to communicate, good reasoning powers, cleverness, attention to detail.
Negative (Debilitated)
Careless, profuse, inconsistent, indecisive, imitative, shiftless, desultory, embarrassed, nervous, rambling, unpoised, un-informed, forgetful, diffusive, shrewd, crafty, artful, untruthful, hypercritical, inquisitive, argumentative, slick, sarcastic, cynical.

VENUS

Key Words — Harmony, Unison

Physical data
Mean diameter : 12,104 km
Rotation speed : 243 days (retrograde)
Sidereal period : 224.7 days
Inclination to orbit : 3.39 degrees
Mean density (water = 1) : 5.2
Surface temperature : 485°C
Mean distance from Sun : 108,200,000 km

Mythology
At first Venus was a Roman goddess of the Spring. However, when she was connected with the Greek goddess Aphrodite she became the goddess of love. Aphrodite was born from the foam caused when Cronus, having castrated Uranus, threw his genitals into the sea. Aphrodite, meaning 'foam born', was fair, beautiful and the grass grew under her soft feet. The legends are many of the strife she caused amongst gods and men as she spread the joys of love throughout the world. Thus she was the source of the frenzy and pain caused by desire.

Astrological data
Rules Taurus and Libra
Exalted in Pisces
Detriment — Aries
Fall — Virgo

Associations
Venus represents the ability to adapt to others, and the nature of one's affections. Its action is to harmonise, beautify, enhance, soften, pacify. It is associated with the power to love, the feelings, the lumbar region, the throat and kidneys. The feminine influence in both sexes, partnerships, possessions,

money, the arts, social life, beauty, adornment, clothes and fashion.

Keywords

Positive (Dignified)
Affectionate, harmonious, chaste, sympathetic, contented, cheerful, graceful, humane, compassionate, refined, companionable, artistic. A gentle manner, tactful, adept in love, appreciative of beauty, having social graces.

Negative (Debilitated)
Lazy, immodest, gushing, disorderly, indecisive, lewd, excessively romantic, emotional, indolent, loud, untidy, thoughtless, gaudy, extravagant, excessive love of pleasure, impractical, weak willed, parasitical.

MARS

Key Words — Energy, Initiative

Physical data
Mean diameter : 6,790 km
Rotation speed : 24 hr 37 mins 23 secs
Sidereal period : 686.9 days
Inclination to orbit : 1.85 degrees
Mean density (water = 1) : 3.9
Day surface temperature –20°C
Night surface temperature : –80°C
Mean distance from sun : 227,940,000 km

Mythology
The Roman god Mars was a paramour of Venus and sire to Romulus and Remus, the forefathers of the Romans. Mars was the god of war but also an agricultural god. Astrologically however, Mars finds connection with the Greek god Ares. The rages of Ares were notorious, his two sons Fear and Fright going

everywhere with him. Seldom successful in battle, he was an equal failure in love.

Astrological data
Rules Aries (Scorpio also but traditional only, now Pluto)
Exalted in Capricorn
Detriment — Libra
Fall — Cancer

Associations
Mars represents passion, desire, energy, courage, assertiveness, initiative. It signifies young men, the armed forces, the police, those that work with fire or metal, butchers, surgeons, athletes. Its action is to energise, intensify, inflame and aggravate. It is connected with the muscular and urogenital systems, gonads, adrenal glands, red blood corpuscles, the kidneys, cuts and burns, the masculine influence in both sexes, aggression, heat, action, weapons, sharp tools, knives and cutting.

Keywords

Positive (Dignified)
Courageous, venturesome, strong, daring, aggressive, energetic, active, fearless, constructive, passionate, decisive, freedom loving, a pioneer, direct approach, a strong leader, a defender of the weak, being strongly sexed, a positive response to situations.

Negative (Debilitated)
Bold, contemptuous, violent, irritable, coarse, audacious, forceful, impulsive, impatient, combative, destructive, sensual, aggressive, irate, brutal, foolhardy, lacking foresight, selfish, quarrelsome, overhasty, indifferent, rude and boisterous.

JUPITER

Key Word — Expansion

Physical data
Mean diameter : 142,700 km
Rotation speed : 9 hrs 51 mins
Sidereal period : 11.86 years
Inclination to orbit : 1.30 degrees
Mean density (water = 1) : 1.3
Surface temperature : –143°C
Mean distance from Sun : 778,300,000 km

Mythology
Jupiter was the god of the sky and weather. The ides of each month were set aside for his worship. He shared a great temple with Juno and Minerva. In time he became connected with the Greek god Zeus. He became the protector of Rome, a warrior that upheld justice, honour and protected the nation's youth. Jupiter had the duty and power to punish men. This he did by hurling thunderbolts. The details of his amorous adventures are many — in one case he turned himself into an eagle in order to seduce Ganymede, a pretty shepherd. He carried her off to become his cupbearer and a constant irritation to Juno.

Astrological data
Rules Sagittarius (Pisces also but traditional only, now Neptune)
Exalted in Cancer
Detriment — Gemini
Fall — Capricorn

Associations
Jupiter represents the higher mind, wisdom, enthusiasm, expansion, expansiveness, optimism, spontaneity and willingness. It signifies the professions, uncles, those connected with the law, the church and universities. It is associated with

knowledge, advanced studies, a philosophical outlook, speculative thinking, religion, the liver, the pituitary gland, foreign countries, languages, book publication and good fortune.

Keywords

Positive (Dignified)
Benevolent, philanthropic, generous, truthful, honest, moral, sincere, charitable, reasonable, compassionate, impartial, optimism, generosity, a sense of justice and compassion, good mental powers, flair for language, good at sport.

Negative (Debilitated)
Prodigal, wasteful, extravagant, pretentious, improvident, dissipated, hypocritical, thriftless, unjust, dishonest, artificial, despotic. Blindly optimistic, self-indulgent, gambling, lawless, conceited, unbalanced beliefs.

SATURN

Key Word — Limitation

Physical data
Mean diameter : 120,000 km
Rotation speed : 10 hrs 14 mins
Sidereal period : 29.46 years
Inclination of orbit : 2.49 degrees
Mean density (water = 1) : 0.7
Surface temperature : –176°C
Mean distance from Sun : 1,427,000,000 km

Mythology
Saturnus was an Italian god of agriculture who lived on earth as a king in the Golden Age. He became associated with the Greek god Cronus, who castrated and overthrew his father Uranus. Saturnalia on 17th December became his main festival, the riotous aspects of our Christmas festivities remaining as a legacy. A hatred or fear of his children was an unfortunate

characteristic inherited by Saturn/Cronus from Uranus. Saturn was entrusted with the guarding of the state treasury and the standards of the Roman Legions.

Astrological data
Rules Capricorn (Aquarius also, but now only traditional)
Exalted in Libra
Detriment — Cancer
Fall — Aries

Associations
Saturn represents concentration, contraction, crystallisation, limitation, self-preservation and ambition. It signifies old or serious people, responsible positions, farmers, builders, civil servants. Its action is to limit, conserve, test, deepen and perfect. It is associated with the teeth, skin, bones, gall bladder, spleen, vagus nerve, crystallisation and acid formation in the joints. It signifies old age, perseverance, tenacity, cold, inevitability, inhibition, restriction and intolerance.

Keywords

Positive (Dignified)
Prudent, contemplative, cautious, serious, precise, persistent, persevering, industrious, provident, patient, economical, reserved, resolute, considerate, mathematical, temperate, chaste, executive, practical, solid, discipline.

Negative (Debilitated)
Skeptical, melancholic, deceitful, incompetent, exacting, avaricious, perverse, indifferent, materialistic, laborious, impotent, repining, acquisitive, secretive, suspicious, fearful, slow, callous, lewd, pessimistic, unreliable, mean, selfish, despondent, severe, aloof, dogmatic, heartless, cruel, hardship.

URANUS

Key Word — Sudden Change

Physical data
Mean diameter : 51,800 km
Rotation speed : 23 hours
Sidereal period : 84 years
Inclination of orbit : 0.8 degrees
Mean density (water = 1) : 1.2
Surface temperature : -216°C
Mean distance from Sun : 2,869,600,000 km

Mythology
Ge or Mother Earth emerged from Chaos and bore Uranus, the starry universe, who became her consort. Uranus made the rain fall on Earth, and from this incestuous union Earth bore all living things. Uranus hated his children, and as they were born hid them away from Earth. She became very angry at this and plotted with Cronus, the eldest son, to remove Uranus. So Earth took Uranus into her bed and whilst Uranus was blind with desire Cronus crept up on them. Taking Uranus in one hand he castrated him with a sickle, throwing the genitals over his shoulder. The blood on the land created the Giants, and the genitals turned the sea to foam, creating Aphrodite (Venus).

Astrological data
Rules Aquarius
Exalted in Scorpio
Detriment — Leo
Fall — Taurus

Associations
Uranus represents originality, inspiration, independence, inventiveness, eccentricity. It signifies unusual people, inventors, electronics and science. Its action is to electrify,

galvanise, shock, awaken, mobilise and innovate suddenly. It is associated with the circulatory system, physical changes, sexual perversion and deviation. Paralysis, cramp, sudden nervous breakdown, modern science, aeronautics, radio, television, space travel and science fiction.

Keywords

Positive (Dignified)
Kind, humanitarian, independent, original, inventive, strong-willed, versatile, ingenious, progressive, reformative, intuitive, metaphysical, unique, unconventional, clairvoyant, magnetic, constructive.

Negative (Debilitated)
Eccentric, abnormal, cranky, perverse, rebellious, unpredictable, erratic, fantastic, extreme, roving, abrupt, premature.

NEPTUNE

Key Word — Nebulousness

Physical data
Mean diameter : 49,000 km
Rotation speed : 22 hours
Sidereal period : 164.8 years
Inclination of orbit : 1.8 degrees
Mean density (water = 1) : 1.6
Surface temperature : –228°C
Mean distance from Sun : 4,498,000,000 km

Mythology
The Roman god Neptune was only a god of fresh water until he was identified with the Greek god Poseidon, the god of the sea. The Roman poets attributed Poseidon's adventures to him and his power and popularity spread. His cult partner was Salacia and his feast day is 23rd July. Poseidon was surly and powerful and he fought alongside Zeus and Hades against the Titans and

the Giants. As a result Zeus became lord of the heavens, Poseidon lord of the seas, and Hades lord of the underworld.

Astrological data
Rules Pisces
Exalted in Leo
Detriment — Virgo
Fall — Aquarius

Associations
Neptune represents intuition, imagination, sensitivity, the ability to transcend boundaries, limitlessness, idealism, expansion of mind, illusion, self-sacrifice and decay. Neptune is associated with the spinal canal, the mental process, the nervous process, the thalamus, drugs, poisons, gas, anaesthetics, matters to do with the sea, prisons, institutions, hospitals, artistic inspiration, spiritual inspiration, mime, poetry, dancing, photography, the cinema and the cinematic arts.

Keywords

Positive (Dignified)
Spiritual, idealistic, inspiration, psychic, psychometric, impressionable, mystical, poetical, musical, subtle, sensitive.
Negative (Debilitated)
Vague, emotional, deceitful, careless, sentimental, diffuse, indecisive, watery, self deception, worrying, vacillating, scheming, obsessional, dreamy, unworldly.

PLUTO

Key Word — Transformation

Physical data
Mean diameter : 2,600 — 3,600 km
Rotation speed : 6.4 days

Sidereal period : 248.5 years
Inclination of orbit : 17.2 degrees
Surface temperature : –233°C
Mean distance from Sun : 5,900,000,000 km

Mythology
Pluto was but another name given to Hades, the god of the underworld. Hades was son of Rhea and Cronus. Hades fought alongside Zeus and Poseidon against the Giants and the Titans. As a reward he was made Lord of the underworld, and given the right to all jewels and precious metals under the earth. His dominion was the land of Tartarus; once entered, nobody left that land of the dead, that place beyond the awful river Styx.

Astrological data
Rules Scorpio
Detriment — Taurus

Associations
Pluto represents those aspects of our character that have not yet been redeemed. It is that part of us that is our own personal underworld. Pluto brings to the surface that which has been hidden in our subconscious, so that it may be transformed into a new source of power. Pluto is associated with the regenerative and creative forces of the body, the unconscious mind and enforced changes. Pluto is connected with the underworld, big business, volcanoes, eruptions, earthquakes, the beginning and end of life.

Keywords

Positive (Dignified)
The Phoenix, the ability to make a fresh start, purifying, regenerative, liberating, incorruptible.
Negative (Debilitated)
Suspicious, destructive, decaying, vicious, sorrowful, suffering, deadly, violent, subconscious, cruel, bestial, sadistic.

Chapter 9

The Houses

'The time has come,' the Walrus said,
   'To talk of many things:
Of shoes-and ships-and sealing wax —
   Of cabbages and Kings —
And why the sea is boiling hot —
   And whether pigs have wings.

Lewis Carroll

The inner circle of the birthchart is divided into twelve sections known as the houses. This inner circle represents the divisions of the earth's surface projected into the sky. To explain their function in the chart is to state that: the planets are the forces that act on us; the signs are how they act; the houses are where they act.

This is how the houses of the chart represent the various facets of our life:

The 1st House
The personality
The appearance
The manner
The outlook on life
The childhood environment

The 2nd House
Possessions
Money and sources of income
Feelings

The 3rd House
Mental activity
Communications, short journeys
Letters and correspondence

Brothers, sisters, cousins, etc.

The 4th House
The home life
Parents
Hereditary characteristics
Beginning and end of life

The 5th House
Creativity
Pleasures, Children
Love Affairs
Sport and recreation

The 6th House
Health
Fitness
The work environment
Subordinates

The 7th House
Marriage
Partnerships
Enemies

The 8th House
Inheritances
Life force elements — sex, birth
Attitudes to death

The 9th House
Long distance travel
Philosophy
Morals and conscience

The 10th House
Ambition and career
Public standing
Outward image and discipline

The 11th House
Social work
Friendships
Clubs, societies

The 12th House
Hospitals or imprisonment
Seclusion or escapism
Accidents or self-sacrifice

NUMEROLOGY

Chapter 10

The Philosophy of Numerology

Omnia in Numeris Sita Sunt
(Everything lies veiled in numbers)

The Structure of Things

A number, is a number, is a number!

That, to the majority, is as far as it goes. A number is simply a symbol denoting a quantity. Yet that quantity so symbolised may denote much more than the mere number that depicts it. For instance in chemistry, two bodies may have an identical number of atoms of the same element, yet still be of an entirely different chemical nature. Take the case of phenylisocyanide and benzotrile: one has an active atom of nitrogen, the other a passive atom of nitrogen, with the result that they are quite different.

So it is with all things. The separate compounds are all drawn from a single base, their differences being due to the domination and proportion of the elements within them.

Search the heavens on any clear night and you may find Mars and Saturn. If you do not it will not be because they are no longer in orbit. They are always in orbit, leastwise they are within our limited knowledge of the Solar system.

So it is in astrology. Mars and Saturn will always be in every person's chart, but their position and aspects will vary from individual to individual. We will all have the Saturnian qualities of melancholy or reservation, just as we all have the Martian qualities of enterprise or aggression. The amount, the type and the nature of those qualities will vary from individual to individual.

Crystallisation takes place according to definite natural laws. The transparent form of crystallised quartz is a body having a characteristic internal structure and enclosed by symmetrically arranged surfaces. It is a thing of beauty. The symmetry and harmony we cannot fail to appreciate, to marvel at.

Just so with the atom. Is not the atom the microcosm and the universe the macrocosm? Are they not identical in structure? From their infinite minuteness to their infinite immenseness, does that not represent the whole of it, the vastness, the range and the totality of it? Yet the wonder is that this vast totality can be reduced to the one unity, the one connecting link, the one purpose, namely — design.

The awareness of this design must leave us in awe, in respect and in reverence to the deity that created it all. For who could claim it to be a mere accident, or just natural evolution. There has to be a deity, a God, an intelligence, for the universe to have such form, such design. Surely then there must be a creator, a God. The universe is but a divine expression, a crystallisation of divine thought in the form of matter.

Man is the fusion of the elements, both terrestrial and cosmic, but there is more to man, there is the energy. Behind the coloured glass there shines the light, the light that is the spirit within all of us. The spirit that *is* all of us. Some might call it character, others the soul.

So it is with the study of numbers. Those impersonal symbols that simply denote a quantity. Numbers are the expression of harmony, of life itself. Just as the law of crystallisation states that metals crystallise at the angles, or complemental angles, of a polygon. So then are they in harmony with each other. As the very structure of crystal denotes the structure of the universe, then does the structure of the atom represent the universe. That very structure must dictate the laws of the universe. It is as Pythagoras states: 'All things are assimilated to number'.

It is by the study of numbers that we learn these laws, this divine expression. From the inception of the universe down to the tiniest aspect of our evolutionary progress. What we call an event is but the re-arrangement of the separate parts in our sphere of reality. Changes that take place in the cosmos are reflected and accompanied by changes in all of its parts. They may produce an uprising, a shower of rain, a war, a rise in the price of cotton. In numerology then we are concerned with the geometry of relationships, with harmonies, with quantities. The symbology is a derivation of these principles.

It has been postulated that Matter is the ultimate expression of spirit, as Form is that of force. Therefore for every spiritual force there is a corresponding spiritual form. Nature becomes an expression of the spiritual world and who could argue with the beauty of the forest on a bright spring morning. The laws governing this spiritual expression can only be found in the relationship of numbers, in the abstract sense of the balance of things. The moral sense is only an awareness of this geometry, and the laws of mind. They arise as part of our evolution, as a function of our growing.

To quote Pythagoras: 'Evolution is the law of life. Number is the law of the Universe. Unity is the law of God.'

Chapter 11

The Origins of Numerology

'I have often admired the mystical way of Pythagoras, and the secret magic of numbers.'

Sir Thomas Browne (1605-82)

The Distant Past

The origins of numerology are lost in the past. It is claimed that one of the earliest of Man's records is on the subject of numerology. Some feel that numerology started with the Atlanteans, others say the Lemurian civilisation was its origin. The ancient Hindus, Assyrians, Babylonians, Chaldeans, Hebrews, Greeks and Romans all had numerological systems and all have doubtless influenced numerology today.

However if any one person can be said to be the father of numerology, then that honour would have to go to Pythagoras. All numerologists would agree that Pythagoras was by far the greatest influence on numerology as practised today.

Pythagoras

Pythagoras was both a brilliant mathematician and profound philosopher; the achievements attributed to him are many. Every child at school knows his famous theorem: 'In a right-angled triangle the square described on the hypotenuse is equal to the sum of the squares on the other two sides.' Known as the theorem of the 47th Proposition, it has been in use now for more than 2,500 years.

Not that the 47th Proposition is the only thing attributed to Pythagoras, or the Pythagorean school. The sacred decad had a particular cosmic significance to them; called the Tetraktys (Fourness) it shows that the sum of $1 + 2 + 3 + 4$ equals 10, or a perfect triangle. Thus:

```
        *
      *   *
    *   *   *
  *   *   *   *
```

Speculation and reflective thought on the matter led to an appreciation of harmonics and numbers, thus when the Tetraktys was applied to musical theory a hidden order of sounds was uncovered. Pythagoras then is credited with the discovery of the relationship between sound and numbers.

Pythagoras saw the Universe as a harmony, a harmonious entity, in which everything emitted a vibration or tone. The vibration of the Universe at a person's moment of birth characterised and gave a signature to their existence from then on. This principle is the foundation stone of all numerology, so to restate it:

> The vibration, tone and harmony of the universe at a person's moment of birth influences both the life and the character of the subject.

Pythagoras — his life

The life of Pythagoras is somewhat surrounded in folklore, especially his birth, which to all accounts bears a striking similarity to that of Christ.

It was prophesied to his mother, by the Oracle at Delphi, that she would bear a son that would outshine all men in beauty and wisdom. Pythagoras was born between 590 and 600BC at Sidon in Phoenicia, his parents travelling at the time. It was even rumoured that the god Apollo was the father. Pythagoras grew up in Samos, but in his late teens started out on his travels. At this time the King of Persia was Cyrus the Great, sometimes known as the people's king. It was because of this ruler's benevolent auspices that Pythagoras was allowed the freedom to travel. It is claimed that he travelled throughout Cyrus's empire and studied under the sages of Egypt, Chaldee, Judea and India.

He was in his sixties when he finally settled in Crotona, in Southern Italy, setting up a school known as the Italic school. He was apparently an awe-inspiring figure who seemed to get stronger with age. He operated the school for some forty years, but unfortunately the people of the town became so afraid of him that he was assassinated. It is said that he lived for more than a hundred years and that at the time of his death he was at the peak of his power. No matter what one might say, his legend has survived remarkably well through the ages.

Philolaus, one of his students, carried on the work after his death and it is said that the great Plato was a student of the Pythagorean principles, but that was to be some seventy years later. Members of the Pythagorean school were expected to observe secrecy and strict loyalty to their order. Because of this much of the teachings have been lost. Only Philolaus and Nichomachus, it seemed, spread the word after the assassination. The members were bound by very strict rules of conduct including sexual purity. They thought that their souls had to be cleansed by music and mental activity.

The Pythagoreans had a proverb which stated: 'All things are assimilated to number'. They were taught that number determines the harmonies of music, and of the spheres, the movement of the Sun, Moon, stars and the proportions of architecture. Pythagoras believed that the world was built on numbers.

Chapter 12

Numerology Today

Man know thyself,
then thou shall know,
the Universe and God.

Pythagoras

The Connections with the Past

For over 2,500 years the systems that Pythagoras developed have been with us, and in all that time the basic concepts are still intact. When you think about it, that is an incredible statement. For 2,500 years we have not advanced the concept — why?

Only a hundred years ago the thought of powered flight was only a dream and less than a hundred years later Man has walked on the Moon. How is it that a set of simple numerology sums have not been improved upon?

The reason, I submit, is that if you already have a core of truth it is very hard to improve upon it.

There are two main systems in use today: the Pythagoras system and the Chaldean system. This book deals in depth with the system of Pythagoras. It would however be of value to briefly discuss Chaldean numerology.

The Chaldean System

The Chaldean system of numerology differs from the accepted western (Pythagorean) system in that it uses only eight numbers and not nine in its determination of the values of the name. The argument put forward is that the Chaldean system relies solely on the vibrational patterns of the letters themselves, and the number values are assigned to those letters on that basis.

I have seen it stated by proponents of the Chaldean system

that the number nine is not used because it has strange properties. If you add nine to itself it remains nine. If you multiply another by nine the answer always reduces to nine. If you add nine to another number, that number after reduction remains the same. The ancients regarded the number nine as holy, therefore it was not used. Today we regard the number nine as the number of humanity; it is the number of man. The Chaldean Alphabet used today is:

The Chaldean Alphabet

1	2	3	4	5	6	7	8
A	B	C	D	E	U	O	F
J	K	G	M	H	V	Z	P
Q		S		X			
Y							

The Pythagoras System

The Pythagoras system combines a number of separate elements derived from the date of birth and the name. These elements together made up a composite picture of the individual. Each element makes its own contribution to the total entity. The proportions that each element contributes are shown below, but it must be emphasised that these proportions are at best only very approximate as they vary from individual to individual, for who is to say one person is more of this or more of that?

The Pythagoras Alphabet

1	2	3	4	5	6	7	8	9
A	B	C	D	E	F	G	H	I
J	K	L	M	N	O	P	Q	R
S	T	U	V	W	X	Y	Z	

One aspect that must be taken into account in this 'Bird's Eye View' is the harmony and balance of the numbers. If the numbers are in harmony, then that person will be in harmony. If the numbers are not in balance then ambivalence and negativity can well result.

In any assessment of character we must bear in mind the words of Virgil (70-19BC), words that have echoed down the centuries: *Non Omnia Possumus Omnes* (We are not all capable of everything).

Chapter 13

The Structure of Numerology

Non Omnia Possumus Omnes
(We are not all capable of everything)

Virgil (70-19BC)

The Bricks and Mortar
There are two foundation stones to the workings of numerology. They are: the date of birth, and the name at birth. There is no debate required about the significance, in numerology, of the date of birth. However there are differing schools of thought about the name. The consensus of opinion is that it is the name we are born with that marks the signature to our life. My personal experience vindicates that view.

From these two foundation stones we can formulate the individual parts that go to make up our individual numerological portfolio.

The Life Path Number
The Life Path Number is the major factor or lesson that has to be achieved or learnt in this life. The Life Path Number is arrived at by the summation of all the numbers in our birthdate. The Life Path Number is the most important of all the numbers.

The Birthday Number
Not as powerful as the Life Path Number the Birthday Number can be said to be a lesser objective in this life. The Birthday Number is the day of the month that we were born. It is any of the numbers between 1 and 31.

The Personality Number
The Personality Number expresses our basic personality, our sexuality. The Personality Number is arrived at by reducing the

Birthday Number to its base form. *Note:* there are no master numbers in the Personality Number.

The Expression Number

The Expression Number defines a person's natural abilities, it demonstrates those characteristics most visible to others. The Expression Number is found by summating the values of all the letters in our name at birth.

The Soul Urge Number

The Soul Urge Number defines a person's inner motivations, his inner drives. The Soul Urge Number is arrived at by summating the value of all the vowels in the name at birth.

The Life Path Modifiers

These are factors in the birthdate that may indicate blocks to our development.

The Intensity Modifiers

These are factors in the overall chart that indicate either blocks or intensification of our abilities.

The Karmic Debt Numbers

These numbers in our chart indicate areas where special attention must be paid to overcome initial limitations to our progress.

The Pythagoras Numbers

This is an analysis of all the numbers in the birthdate. It shows the potential and the limitation of the numbers, both present and missing in the birthdate.

The Pythagoras Cross

This simple cross demonstrates a person's capabilities, potentials, sensitivities and limitations. The Cross is always shown as follows, the number of the birthdate being inserted appropriately.

3	6	9
2	5	8
1	4	7

For example, Mrs Nancy Reagan, born 6th July 1923. Her numbers would be inserted thus:

3	6	9
2		
1		7

Birthdate
numbers
1, 2, 3,
6, 7, 9

The format of the cross enables the Pythagoras Planes, or action lines, to be identified.

The Numerology Calculations

The Life Path Number
The greatest single factor of a person's numerology is their Life Path Number. We arrive at this number by summating the birthday numbers:

Step 1
Reduce the person's birthdate to numbers. Take the baseball player Joe DiMaggio as an example, date of birth 25th November, 1914.

25 / 11 / 1914

Step 2

Now we must reduce the day, the month and the year to single
numbers. However, there are two master numbers that are never
reduced. These are 11 and 22. So if the person was born on the 11th or
the 22nd or during November, leave those numbers alone for the
moment.

The date	25	/ 11 /	1914
becomes	(2+5)	11	(1+9+1+4)
becomes	7	11	15

Step 3

Now we must reduce these numbers again to get a number with a
single digit, i.e. 9 or less. However, if they are master numbers, 11 or
22, then leave them as they are.

The date	25	/ 11 /	1914
becomes	(2+5)	11	(1+9+1+4)
becomes	7	11	15
becomes	7	11	(1+5)
becomes	7	11	6

Step 4

Now we must add together the final numbers of each group thus.

The date	25	/ 11 /	1914
becomes	(2+5)	11	(1+9+1+4)
becomes	7	11	15
becomes	7	11	(1+5)
becomes	7	11	6
becomes	7	+ 11 + 6 = 24	

Step 5

If the result is a master number, 11 or 22, then that is the life
path number. However, if it is not and it is greater than 9 then
we must reduce it again thus:

The date	25	/ 11 /	1914
becomes	(2+5)	11	(1+9+1+4)
becomes	7	11	15
becomes	7	11	(1+5)
becomes	7	11	16
becomes	7	+ 11 + 6 = 24	
becomes	2	+ 4 = 6	

Joe DiMaggio's Life Path Number is 6.

One may now refer to the Life Path Number 6 in the references.

The above looks complicated but it is really very simple. Let's take a look at some more celebrities and see if you can follow the working.

Frank Sinatra — Date of birth 12th December, 1917

The date	12	/ 12 /	1917
becomes	3	3	18
becomes	3	3	9
becomes	3	+ 3 + 9 = 15	
becomes	1	+ 5 = 6	

Frank Sinatra's Life Path Number is 6

Gough Whitlam — Date of birth 11th July, 1917. (*Note:* the day number is a master number and is left)

The date	11	/ 7 /	1917
becomes	11	7	18
becomes	11	7	9
becomes	11	+ 7 + 9 = 27	
becomes	2	+ 7 = 9	

Mr Gough Whitlam's Life Path Number is 9

President Ronald Reagan — Date of birth 6th February, 1911

The date	6	/ 2 /	1911
becomes	6	2	12
becomes	6	2	3
becomes	6	+ 2 + 3 = 11 (a master number)	

President Reagan's Life Path Number is 11

Junie Morosi — Date of birth 26th July, 1933

The date	26	/ 7 /	1933
becomes	8	7	16
becomes	8	7	7
becomes	8	+ 7 + 7 = 22 (a master number)	

Junie Morosi's Life Path Number is 22

Billy Jean King — Date of birth 22nd November, 1943. (*Note:* both day and month numbers are master numbers, so are left until the final addition)

The date	22	/ 11 /	1943
becomes	22	11	17
becomes	22	11	8
becomes	22	+ 11 + 8 = 41	
becomes	4	+ 1 = 5	

Billy Jean King's Life Path Number is 5

Why is it done this way? By this method the master numbers emerge correctly. Also we determine if Life Path Modifiers exist. Lastly, we can check for Karmic Debts in the numbers. Up to this point we have not complicated the Life Path calculations with Karmic Numbers. The examples following show how the Karmic Numbers may be handled.

Karmic Numbers in the Life Path

It is believed that Karmic Numbers signify problems that can be expected in this life as a result of misapplied energies in the past. The existence of a Karmic Number indicates a Karmic debt. Whether you believe in reincarnation or not the Karmic debt in a birthdate cannot easily be ignored.

The Karmic Numbers are 13 — 14 — 16 — 19. A full description of their significance can be found in the reference section. In the calculation of the Life Path Number the Karmic Number should be identified as shown below.

Anna Magnani, date of birth 7th March, 1908

The date	7	/ 3/	1908
becomes	7	3	18
becomes	7	3	9
becomes	7	+ 3 + 9 = 19	

Anna Magnani's Life Path Number is 19/1
Anna has a Karmic Debt of 19 in the Life Path

George Murphy, date of birth 4th July, 1902

The date	4	/ 7 /	1902
becomes	4	7	12
becomes	4	7	3
becomes	4	+ 7 + 3 = 14	

George Murphy's Life Path Number is 14/5
George has a Karmic Debt of 14 in the Life Path

Jack Palance, date of birth 18th February, 1919

The date	18	/ 2 /	1919
becomes	9	2	20
becomes	9	2	2
becomes	9	+ 2 + 2 = 13	

Jack Palance's Life Path Number is 13/4
Jack has a Karmic Debt of 13 in the Life Path

Note: the expression of Karmic Numbers and Master Numbers follows the pattern of showing the Karmic or Master Number first then the reduced value afterwards. The individual is given the choice as to the path they choose. However, for Karmic Numbers there would not seem to be much of a choice!

Example : 13/4 ; 22/4 ; 16/7 ; 19/1 ; 11/2 ; 14/5 etc.

The Life Path Modifier.

The Life Path Modifier is a factor within the calculation of the Life Path Number that indicates a person could have blocks to their development of character. The indicators are the repeated appearance of identical numbers within the Life Path calculation.

1. If the reduced day or month numbers equal each other, or equal the reduced year number, a modifier is in force.
2. If the reduced day, month or year numbers equal the Life Path Number or reduced Life Path Number, a more severe modifier is in force.
3. Any combination of 1 and 2 above.

These Life Path Modifiers can cause the person to start out in life expressing only the negative aspects of their potential. As a result their development as individuals is impaired. In some cases this has resulted in people ignoring their potential until quite late in life.

Let us look at such an example — we will call him Charlie Spinks, date of birth 17th August, 1956. Remember our calculation procedure:

The date	17	/ 8 /	1956
becomes	(1+7)	8	(1+9+5+6)
becomes	8	8	21
becomes	8	8	(2+1)
becomes	8	8	3

Stop here! The day number and the month number have reduced to be the same value. When this occurs the person can experience a block to his development. To continue with Charlie's chart:

becomes	8	+ 8 + 3 = 19
becomes	1	+ 9 + 10
becomes	1	+ 0 = 1

Charlie's Life Path Number is 1.

Let us now look at a more aggravated case of the Life Path Modifier. We will call this person Fred Daggs, date of birth 13th July, 1903. Remember our calculation procedure:

The date	13	/ 7 /	1903
becomes	(1+3)	7	(1+9+3) 13
becomes	4	+ 7 +	(1+3)
becomes	4	+ 7 + 4 = (1+5) = 6	

Fred's Life Path Number is 6

Stop here! The reduced day number and the year number are effectively the same. This can result in a delay of many years before Fred reaches his full potential.

Let us now look at a more aggravated case of the Life Path Modifier. We will call this person Will Jones, date of birth 16th June, 1947. Remember our calculation procedure.

The date	16	/ 6 /	1947
becomes	(1+6)	6	(1+9+4+7)
becomes	7	6	21
becomes	7	6	(2+1)
becomes	7	+ 6 + 3 = 16	
becomes	1	+ 6 = 7	

Will's Life Path Number is 7.

Stop here! The reduced day number and the Life Path Number are identical. This indicates a more severe block than the first example.

Finally let us look at an example of a double block. We will call this person John Nick, date of birth 9th April, 1935. Remember our calculation procedure:

The date	9	/ 4 /	1935
becomes	9	4	(1+9+3+5)
becomes	9	4	18
becomes	9	4	(1+8)
becomes	9	4	9 = 22

John's Life Path Number is 22.

Stop here! There are two blocks in this example. The first occurs as a result of the reduced day number equalling the reduced year number. The second block occurs because the month number equals the reduced life path number. Remember all master numbers have to be worked at or else the subject reverts to the single digit. This subject did not start to experience a change in his life until well past 50 years of age.

The Lesson.

The lesson is not to think that a block cannot be overcome. Anything in numerology can be overcome! The lesson is to be aware of ourselves, to identify our problems and in so doing use fully this wonderful gift we call life.

The Birthday Number

The Birthday Number can be considered to be intrinsically part of the Life Path Number. It expresses another point of view of our target for achievement. For example, Salvador Dali was born on 11th March, 1904. His Life Path Number was 1 — very much an individual — as were his paintings. The Birthday Number of 11 allies a spiritual and mystical connotation to the life direction, as amply demonstrated by his paintings.

The Birthday Number is not reduced therefore it can be any number between one and thirty-one.

The Personality Number

The Personality Number is a reduced version of the Birthday Number. The Personality Number expresses the fundamentals and basics of a person, their attitude, their sexuality. The Personality Number expresses aspects not covered by the Birthday Number description.

The Personality Number does not have master numbers in its format.

Take Joe DiMaggio again:
Date of birth —   25/11/1914
Birthday Number   25
Therefore Personality Number   2 + 5 = 7

Or Frank Sinatra:
Date of birth —   12/12/1917
Birthday Number   12
Therefore Personality Number   1 + 2 = 3

Or Gough Whitlam:
Date of Birth —   11/7/1917
Birthday Number   11
Therefore Personality Number   1 + 1 = 2

Or Junie Morosi:
Date of Birth —   26/7/1933
Birthday Number   26
Therefore Personality Number   2 + 6 = 8

Or Billy Jean King:
Date of Birth —   22/11/1943
Birthday Number   22
Therefore personality Number   2 + 2 = 4

The Expression Number

The Expression Number defines those abilities latent in a person. It is the second in significance of the numerology elements. All of us have been given various gifts and talents. The Expression Number in describing these talents shows that part of us which is visible to others.

The Expression characteristics are so visible that they are often mistaken for the essence of a person. The Expression Number directs us to those abilities we use every day, that part of us the world sees.

The Alphabet

1	2	3	4	5	6	7	8	9
A	B	C	D	E	F	G	H	I
J	K	L	M	N	O	P	Q	R
S	T	U	V	W	X	Y	Z	

Example: Let us take George Bernard Shaw as an example.

Step 1

Lay-out the full name and beneath it place the number value of the letters.

```
G E O R G E    B E R N A R D    S H A W
7 5 6 9 7 5    2 5 9 5 1 9 4    1 8 1 5
```

Step 2

Add the numbers of each name together *separately*. Then reduce those numbers to a single digit, or master number.

$$\text{GEORGE} \quad 7 + 5 + 6 + 9 + 7 + 5 \qquad = 39$$
$$= 3 + 9 = 12$$
$$= 1 + 2 = \ \ 3$$

$$\text{BERNARD} \quad 2 + 5 + 9 + 5 + 1 + 9 + 4 = 35$$
$$= 3 + 5 = 8$$

$$\text{SHAW} \quad 1 + 8 + 1 + 5 \qquad\qquad = 15$$
$$= 1 + 5 = 6$$

Step 3

Add the numbers calculated for each name. Reduce them to a single digit, karmic number or master number.

$$3 + 8 + 6 = 17$$
$$1 + 7 = 8$$

The Expression Number for George Bernard Shaw is 8

Step 4

On a numerological chart the calculation would be arranged so

$$
\begin{array}{ccc}
\text{G E O R G E} & \text{B E R N A R D} & \text{S H A W} \\
7\ 5\ 6\ 9\ 7\ 5 & 2\ 5\ 9\ 5\ 1\ 9\ 4 & 1\ 8\ 1\ 5 \\
\end{array}
$$

$$(39)\ 3 \quad + \quad (35)\ 8 \quad + \quad (15)\ 6 = 17 = 8\ \textit{Expression}$$

Let us take a few more examples of the expression number:

Example One

$$
\begin{array}{cc}
\text{A L B E R T} & \text{E I N S T E I N} \\
1\ 3\ 2\ 5\ 9\ 2 & 5\ 9\ 5\ 1\ 2\ 5\ 9\ 5 \\
\end{array}
$$

$$(22)\ 22 \quad + \quad (41)\ 5 \qquad = 27 = 9\ \textit{Expression}$$

Example Two

$$
\begin{array}{cc}
\text{J U L I E} & \text{A N D R E W S} \\
1\ 3\ 3\ 9\ 5 & 1\ 5\ 4\ 9\ 5\ 5\ 1 \\
\end{array}
$$

$$(21)\ 3 \quad + \quad (30)\ 3 \qquad = 6\ \textit{Expression}$$

Example Three

$$
\begin{array}{cc}
\text{I R V I N G} & \text{B E R L I N} \\
9\ 9\ 4\ 9\ 5\ 7 & 2\ 5\ 9\ 3\ 9\ 5 \\
\end{array}
$$

$$(43)\ 7 \quad + \quad (33)\ 6 \qquad = 13/4 = 4\ \textit{Expression}$$
$$13\ \textit{Karmic Debt}$$

Example Four

$$
\begin{array}{cc}
\text{H A R O L D} & \text{W I L S O N} \\
8\ 1\ 9\ 6\ 3\ 4 & 5\ 9\ 3\ 1\ 6\ 5 \\
\end{array}
$$

$$(31)\ 4 \quad + \quad (29)\ 11 \qquad = 15 = 6\ \textit{Expression}$$

Example Five

$$
\begin{array}{cc}
\text{S Y L V I A} & \text{S N Y D E R} \\
1\ 7\ 3\ 4\ 9\ 1 & 1\ 5\ 7\ 4\ 5\ 9 \\
\end{array}
$$

$$(25)\ 7 \quad + \quad (31)\ 4 \qquad = 11 = \textit{Expression}$$

The Soul Urge Number

The Soul Urge Number defines a person's inner desires. It shows what he wants to be, what he wants to have and what he wants to do.

The Soul Urge is third in importance of the core elements in numerology. Sometimes called the Heart's Desire, the Soul Urge is concerned with our motivation and our drives. It shows our longings and our secret desires. It expresses those things that are important to us, that which drives our emotions.

The Soul Urge is derived by finding the sum of the vowels in our name at birth. Follow the procedure below:

The Alphabet

1	2	3	4	5	6	7	8	9
A	B	C	D	E	F	G	H	I
J	K	L	M	N	O	P	Q	R
S	T	U	V	W	X	Y	Z	

Notes on Vowels:

1 A, E, I, O, U are always vowels.
2 There is at least one vowel in every syllable.
3 Y is sometimes a vowel. It is a vowel when there is no other vowel.
4 Y is a vowel when it is preceded by A, E, I, O or U and is sounded as one sound.
5 W can be a vowel. It is a vowel when it is preceded by A, E, I, O or U and is sounded as one sound.

Example: Let us take George Bernard Shaw as an example:

Step 1
Lay-out the full name and above it place the number value of the vowels. (*Note:* the 'W' in Shaw is considered to be a vowel.)

```
 5 6      5       5      1            1 5
G E O R G E   B E R N A R D   S H A W
```

Step 2
Add the numbers of each name together *separately*. Then reduce those numbers to a single digit, or master number.

GEORGE	5 + 6 + 5	= 16 = 1 + 6 = 7
BERNARD	5 + 1	= 6
SHAW	5 + 1	= 6

Step 3
Add the numbers calculated for each name. Reduce them to a single

digit, karmic number or master number.

$7 + 6 + 6 = 19$

The Soul Urge Number for George Bernard Shaw is 19/1
George Bernard Shaw has a Soul Urge Karmic Number 19

Step 4

On a numerological chart the calculation would be arranged so:

(16) 7   6   6

| 5 6 | 5 | 5 | 1 | 1 | = 19/1 Soul Urge |

G E O R G E   B E R N A R D   S H A W   *19 Karmic Soul Urge*

The Pythagorean Alphabets

The English language alphabet of 26 letters has its number values assigned by the position of the letter in the alphabet. Despite the critics the system definitely works and works very well.

The English and French languages use 26 letters. Here is the alphabet.

1	2	3	4	5	6	7	8	9
A	B	C	D	E	F	G	H	I
J	K	L	M	N	O	P	Q	R
S	T	U	V	W	X	Y	Z	

However, not all of us were born in English-speaking countries. If you are of Spanish descent, here is the Spanish alphabet of 28 letters.

1	2	3	4	5	6	7	8	9
A	B	C	D	E	F	G	H	I
				N				
J		L	M	Ñ	O	P	Q	R
								RR
S	T	U	V	W	X	Y	Z	
	CH			LL				

Lastly, if you are of Italian origin here is the 21 letter Italian alphabet.

1	2	3	4	5	6	7	8	9
A	B	C	D	E	F	G	H	I
		L	M	N	O	P	Q	R
S	T	U	V				Z	

Please refer to these last two alphabets when working with names of Hispanic or Italian origins.

The Pythagoras Numbers

The use of the Pythagoras Cross is a simple method of analysing a person's abilities and limitations. The method used is to place a person's birthdate into a matrix and then analyse each group of numbers separately. The Cross is always set out this way:

3	6	9
2	5	8
1	4	7

Example: Mr Gough Whitlam — Born 11th July, 1916. His numbers would be inserted thus:

	6	9
1111		7

Birthdate numbers
1,1,1,1
6,7,9

This now shows us that Mr Whitlam has:

        the number 1 has four
        the number 2 is missing
        the number 3 is missing
        the number 4 is missing
        the number 5 is missing
        the number 6 has one
        the number 7 has one
        the number 8 is missing
        the number 9 has one

The interpretations of these number combinations may now be referred to. It must be pointed out that not only do the positive quantity numbers have interpretations but also the missing numbers must be read as well.

The Pythagoras Cross is not only set out to assess the quantities of the numbers. In the section 'The Pythagoras Planes' you will see we use this format to assess the potential of a person's action lines or planes — called the Pythagoras Planes.

The Pythagoras Planes

These are the lines of force that appear when the Pythagoras Cross is implemented. They describe aspects of a person's character. In Mrs Reagan's case they would appear thus:

* **3*	*6*	*9**	Birthdate numbers
			1,2,3
			6,7,9
* 2 *			
* 1 *		7	

As shown, they are the lines that have all been completed by numbers just as if you had been playing a game of Tic Tac Toe, or Noughts and Crosses.

The two lines that have been completed in Mrs Reagan's chart are:

the 3,6,9 line which we call the Plane of Empathy.

the 1,2,3 line which we call the Plane of Thought.

These Planes may now be referred to in the references.

Below are listed all the 'Positive' Pythagoras Planes

```
  3  |  6  |  9
-----|-----|-----
  2  |  5  |  8
-----|-----|-----
  1  |  4  |  7
```

The Numbers	*The Pythagoras Planes*
1 : 2 : 3	The Plane of Thought
4 : 5 : 6	The Plane of Tenacity
7 : 8 : 9	The Plane of Energy
1 : 4 : 7	The Plane of Dexterity
2 : 5 : 8	The Plane of Passion
3 : 6 : 9	The Plane of Empathy
3 : 5 : 7	The Plane of Insight
1 : 5 : 9	The Plane of Purpose

Note: As well as positive number planes, the missing numbers also have planes.

The Free Number Planes

Not only do we look for lines that have all their numbers filled in the Pythagoras Cross, we must also look for empty lines. Called Free Number Planes, these planes have equal significance to their complete number counterparts.

Let's take the case of another literary figure, Harriet Beecher Stowe, born 14th June, 1811.

* * 6		
2	* * * 8	
1111	4	* * *

Birthday numbers
1,1,1,1
4,6,8

In this case all the numbers have been included and it has left a blank line on what would have been the 3,5 and 7 squares. (See diagram).

This free number plane is called the Plane of Vision. The attributes of this plane are a duality which on the one hand can indicate great visionary powers, or conversely great skepticism.

The Free Number Planes are:

3	6	9
2	5	8
1	4	7

Free Numbers	*The Pythagoras Planes*
4 : 5 : 6	The Plane of Saturn
7 : 8 : 9	The Plane of Dedication
1 : 4 : 7	The Plane of Perception
2 : 5 : 8	The Plane of Sensitivity

3 : 6 : 9	The Plane of Inspiration
3 : 5 : 7	The Plane of Vision
1 : 5 : 9	The Plane of Development

Note: the line 1 : 2 : 3 has not been completed, as people having all these numbers missing will not be born until the year 4000!

Putting it All Together

So far we have seen how to calculate the individual parts of a numerology analysis. Let us now see how it goes together.

Example: Let us take George Bernard Shaw born 26th July, 1856.

Date of birth   26 / 7 / 1856

$$8 + 7 + (20) 2 = (17) = 8 \; Life \; Path$$

$$26 \qquad\qquad\qquad = 26 \; Birthday$$

$$8 \; Personality$$

(16) 7	6	6	= 19/1 Soul Urge
5 6 5	5 1	1 5	
G E O R G E	B E R N A R D	S H A W	
7 5 6 9 7 5	2 5 9 5 1 9 4	1 8 1 5	
(30) 3 +	(35) 8 +	(15) 6	= 8 *Expression*

However, before we can refer to the reference section for the character descriptions, we must first consider the 'Intensity Modifiers' and 'The Aspects'.

	66	
**2*	*5*	*8**
1		7

Birthdate numbers
1,2,5,6,
6,7,8

From the Pythagoras analysis George Bernard Shaw has:

the number 1 has four
the number 2 has one
the number 3 is missing
the number 4 is missing
the number 5 has one
the number 6 has two
the number 7 has one
the number 8 has one
the number 9 is missing

The Intensity Modifiers

The example just given for George Bernard Shaw is a good case of the Intensity Modifier in action.

From the chart we can see that not only did a block exist in the birthdate numbers, but also the Expression Number was the same as that of the Lifepath Number and the Birthday Number.

The Intensity Modifier principle works on the basis that if two elements (i.e. Life Path and Expression) are the same value then the subject will probably start out in life expressing the negative extremes of their potential rather than their positive aspects. Once a person is aware, he is free to release his positive energies to the full. However, in the case of Mr Shaw one only has to look at the prodigity of his writings to see how he turned this positive potential to such great purpose. One quote I have heard about Shaw was, 'You name it he wrote it'.

The 8's in his chart attest to his organisation, and rigid attitudes to work. Personally I will always have a picture of a straight-backed man, with a lot to say, and a wonderful way of saying it.

The Intensity Modifiers can be turned to our advantage, we have only to realise our potential.

One saying that I feel fits this case is: 'We are never given more than we can handle'. How true that was of George Bernard Shaw.

Summary

An Intensity Modifier can be considered to be effective if:

1 The Life Path Number equals the Birthday/Personality Number
2 The Life Path Number equals the Expression Number
3 The Life Path Number equals the Soul Urge Number
4 The Expression Number equals the Birthday/Personality Number
5 The Expression Number equals the Soul Urge Number
6 The Soul Urge Number equals the Birthday/Personality Number

Example

Another example of the Intensity Modifier principle in action was Martin Luther King (Michael Luther King), born 15th January, 1929. Martin Luther King had a 5 Expression and a 5 Soul Urge. A brilliant leader of the Civil Rights Movement in the USA, King worked all his life to prove the rights of the individual and of freedom. The 5 signifies the constructive use of freedom. I can think of no better example of the Intensity Modifier being turned to the good of all. Moreover I can think of no better example of the principles of numerology being demonstrated so effectively as in the case of Martin Luther King and the energy of the 5, the energy of freedom.

The Aspects of the Numbers

The aspects that numbers form with each other is a matter at the heart of numerology. If a person has a life path number 1 and an expression number 2 it must be expected that the individuation of the 1 will clash with the submissiveness of the 2 — they are in discord. The chart which follows identifies the aspects numbers form with each other. In the sketch, three street cars symbolise the three main facets of our numerological

The Aspects

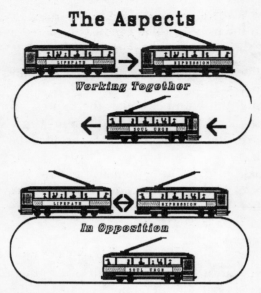

makeup. They are 'Life Path', 'Expression' and 'Soul Urge'. The street cars are connected by three tracks, these tracks representing the aspects.

Using George Bernard Shaw again let us substitute the values for 'Life Path', 'Expression', and 'Soul Urge'. Referring to the chart we see that 8 and 8 are Intensity Modifiers and therefore in discord. We can note discord in the track connecting 'Life Path' and 'Expression'. Looking again at the chart we note that 9 and 1 are in harmony, the remaining two tracks can now be so noted.

That is all there is to it, yet the picture is now much clearer when we make our final delineation of the numerological character. The individual parts of the analysis may now be combined. The complete analysis is best written out and an appropriate note made where aspects, karmic numbers or intensity modifiers change the emphasis of the reading.

For those so interested, at the end of this book are listed over 700 celebrities and their birthdays. Maybe you might wish to while away a wet Sunday afternoon. Good Luck.

The Numerology Calculations
Putting it All Together
The Aspects Chart

	1	2	3	4	5	6	7	8	9	11	22
1	IM	D	H	V	D	D	H	D	D	D	D
2	D	IM	H	H	D	H	D	D	H	H	D
3	H	H	IM	D	H	H	D	D	H	H	D
4	H	H	D	IM	D	H	H	D	D	D	V
5	V	D	H	D	IM	D	D	D	D	D	D
6	D	H	H	H	D	IM	D	D	H	H	H
7	D	D	D	H	D	D	IM	D	D	H	D
8	H	D	D	D	D	D	D	IM	D	D	H
9	D	H	H	D	D	H	D	D	IM	H	H
11	D	H	H	D	D	H	H	D	H	IM	D
22	D	D	D	V	D	H	D	H	H	D	IM

H = Harmonious; D = Discordant; IM = Intensity Modifer;
V = Variable.

Chapter 14

Numerology Reference

THE LIFE PATH NUMBERS

THE NUMBER 1

Keywords — Independence . . . Attainment

Focus

A — *The achievement and attainment of independence.*
B — *The application of independence in leadership*
C — *Independence as a source of creativity.*

Characteristics
* Leadership capability
* Much inner strength
* Executive ability and organisational skills
* Good potential for achievement and reward
* Self-centred

Positive factors
Creation, originality, independence, courage, progress, ambition, positiveness, willpower, leadership, pioneering, activity, force.

Negative factors
Laziness, imitation, dependence, selfishness, instability, egotism, weakness, fear, bravado, contrariness, stagnation, stubbornness.

Destructive factors

Tyranny, antagonism, iconoclasm, bullying, self first and self last.

Commentary

The Life Path 1 is focused on the need to individuate. The identity of the self is paramount. Much of the formative years may be spent in a dependent role, the person becoming frustrated with their lot. Once this dependence has been handled properly the individual may develop into a full balanced personality that has great potential for leadership, reward and satisfaction.

Examples

Charlie Chaplin, Maurice Chevalier, Sean Connery, Gene Autry, Karl Marx, Leo Tolstoy

THE NUMBER 2

Keywords — Relation ... Co-Operation

Focus

A   — *The satisfaction of contributing in a group.*
B   — *The use of persuasion rather than force.*
C   — *To be content to be the power behind the throne.*

Characteristics

*   Much sensitivity to others' feelings
*   Works well with others — co-operative
*   Shows much consideration for others

*   Not concerned with material status

*   Expresses and receives love — a good friend

Positive factors

Love, service, gentleness, harmony, adaptability, charm, diplomacy, friendliness, rhythm, music, receptivity, co-operation, consideration of others.

Negative factors

Vacillation, apathy, indifference, shyness, self-effacement, oversensitivity, spinelessness, sycophantic, sulkiness, discontent, slackness, carelessness.

Destructive factors

Deception, mischief-making, sullenness, cruelty, cowardice, bad temper, slyness, lying, pessimism.

Commentary

The Life Path 2 is concerned with the sublimation of the self into co-operative ventures. Be it a marriage, the family or external social groups, the Life Path 2 people are often the hard-working individuals, always just behind the scenes. They have to control and balance their sensitivity, as they are prone to always having their feelings hurt. Having much sensitivity to others they can be a lover, a friend or a diplomat in the finest sense.

Examples

Gustav Mahler, Frederick Delius

THE NUMBER 3

Keywords — Expression ... Joy of Living

Focus

A — *To express the joy of living.*

B — *To appreciate and communicate the beauty in the world.*

C — *To practise artistic and creative self-expression.*

Characteristics

* A warm and friendly personality
* Sociable, an asset to any social group
* Interesting and makes good conversation
* Has a talent with words, writing, speaking, singing
* Much creative imagination

Positive factors

Artistic expression, joy of living, freedom from worry, optimism, inspiration, talent, imagination, good taste, sociability, friendliness, kindness.

Negative factors

Worry, whining, dilettantism, criticism, gossip, extravagance, vanity, triviality, superficiality, exaggeration.

Destructive factors

Jealousy, hypocrisy, wastefulness, cowardice, intolerance.

Commentary

The Life Path 3 people have been given many talents. A sunny disposition and a positive approach to life makes them welcome additions to any social group. They accept the existence of problems yet seem to deal with them without being dragged down into a morass of worrying. Even when things are difficult and tough the 3s' optimism and brightness shines through. They may mature later than other Life Path Numbers.

Examples

Bing Crosby, Judy Garland, Gina Lollobrigida, Gloria Swanson, Dana Andrews, Queen Victoria.

THE NUMBER 4

Keywords — Limitation ... Order ... Service Focus

Focus

A — *To learn the advantage of order and system.*
B — *To accept the down-to-earth and the mundane.*
C — *To live in harmony with his limitations.*

Characteristics
* Practical and down-to-earth
* Systematic and organised
* Capable and willing to work long and hard
* Honest, sincere and has a serious approach to life
* Rigid attitude and a fixed approach to life

Positive factors
Practicality, service, patience, exactitude, organisation, application, devotion, patriotism, conservatism, pragmatism, dignity, economy, trust, worthiness, endurance, loyalty.

Negative factors
Plodding, narrowness, exaction, repression, minuteness, clumsiness, dogmatism, crudeness, brusqueness, restriction, rigidity, sternness, dullness.

Destructive factors
Vulgarity, animalism, hatred, violence, jealousy, inhumanity, resistance, destruction, cruelty.

Commentary
The Life Path 4 people have to learn to live life with limitation. At first this can be exceedingly frustrating, but they adapt to

their circumstances and then progress. Once this lesson is learned the life of the Life Path 4 person can be both satisfying and rewarding.

Examples

Jane Russell, Sigmund Freud, Percy Bysshe Shelley, Andre Previn, Thor Heyerdahl.

THE NUMBER 5

Keywords — Constructive Freedom

Focus

A — *To use freedom constructively.*
B — *To control restlessness and impatience.*
C — *To learn to profit from experience.*

Characteristics
* Versatile and active
* Clever, able to complete what they start
* Restless and impatient
* Loves change, wants to travel
* Good friends and companions

Positive factors
Freedom, progress, versatility, understanding, variety, adaptability, curiosity, experience, cleverness, unattachment, sociability, change, travel, adventure, companionship.

Negative factors
Irresponsibility, procrastination, carelessness, self indulgence, thoughtlessness, inconsistency, sensationalism, bad taste.

Destructive factors
Libertinism, perversion, abuse of freedom, alcoholism, drug addiction, sensuality.

Commentary
The Life Path 5 people have to find the constructive use of freedom. Very often gifted in many ways they have to find the path that is for them the most satisfying. Restless and impatient they run the risk of frittering their life away in pointless pursuits. They must find the activity and the path that will ultimately reward them the most, that reward not necessarily being measured in material terms.

Examples
Sebastian Cabot, Ursula Andress, Lauren Bacall, James Joyce, Mao Tse Tung, Anton Dvorak.

THE NUMBER 6

Keywords — Balance . . . Responsibility . . . Love

Focus
A — *To learn the satisfaction of being responsible.*
B — *To know the pleasure of giving comfort to others.*
C — *To seek balance and harmony in life.*

Characteristics
* Very responsible people
* Loving and appreciative of others
* Sympathetic, kind and generous

*   Loves children, can be a good teacher
*   Loves the home and family

Positive factors

Love, harmony, home, responsibility, adjustment, musical talent, sympathy, understanding, domesticity, guardianship, stability, poise, protection, healing, firmness, balance, idealism, conscientiousness, justice, service to mankind.

Negative factors

Anxiety, worry, meddlesomeness, misplaced sympathy, mistaken ideals, interference, conventionality, pride, smugness, unwilling service, drudgery, despondency.

Destructive factors

Cynicism, egotism, suspicion, jealousy, slavery, domestic tyranny.

Commentary

The Life Path 6 people find great reward in caring for others, usually in their own family circle. The Life Path 6 people give out love and appreciation to all. Very often the pivot of the home, they harmonise all around them into the unit we know as the family.

Examples

Peter Ustinov, Henrik Ibsen, Elizabeth Barrett Browning, Leonard Bernstein, Maurice Ravel, Giuseppe Verdi.

THE NUMBER 7

Keywords — Analysis ... Understanding

Focus

A — *To understand themselves.*
B — *To seek peace of mind.*
C — *To seek wisdom and understanding.*

Characteristics

* Reserved people, they are difficult to get to know
* They operate on a different 'wave length' from most of us
* Introspective and thoughtful
* Self sufficient, confident in their abilities
* Not adaptable, somewhat rigid in their ways

Positive factors

Mental analysis, technicality, introspection, peace, poise, research, spirituality, faith, trust, stoicism, refinement, wisdom, understanding, silence, fundamentals.

Negative factors

Melancholy, fault finding, sarcasm, coldness, aloofness, skepticism, confusion, humiliation, nervousness, erraticism.

Destructive factors

Faithlessness, turbulence, drink, malice, suppression, deceitfulness, theft, cheating, craftiness.

Commentary

The Life Path 7 people have to know the meaning and reasons behind things. They may be teachers, researchers or scientists. They are drawn to understanding themselves and the world around them. Too often they fight against those things they could understand the best. Sometimes they fail to get the spiritual message, leaving them lost and apathetic.

Examples

Peter Sellers, Richard Attenborough, Nikolai Lenin, Frederick Chopin, Peter Ilyitch Tchaikovsky, Yul Brynner.

THE NUMBER 8

Keywords — Material satisfaction

Focus

A — *To know the satisfaction of the material world.*
B — *To seek power and mastery.*
C — *To seek position and status in life.*

Characteristics
* Efficient and energetic
* Ambitious and self-confident
* Executive ability, organisational skills
* A good judge of character
* Tendency to rigidity and stubbornness

Positive factors
Power, authority, success, material freedom, judgement, discrimination, executive ability, organisation, leadership, management, practicality, thoroughness, dependability, self reliance, control, the will to succeed.

Negative factors
Strain, hardness, materialism, intolerance, self interest, worry, scheming, carelessness, love of power, impatience, poor judgement.

Destructive factors
Abuse of power, revenge, oppressiveness, injustice, cruelty, unscrupulousness, domineering.

Commentary

The Life Path 8 people are here to succeed in this world. They are equipped to progress and prosper in the material world. Ideally suited to business, they make excellent managers and executives. They have the practicality, the insight and the confidence to make good business decisions.

Examples

Laurence Olivier, Ginger Rogers, Darryl F. Zanuck, George Bernard Shaw, Artur Rubinstein, John Philip Sousa.

THE NUMBER 9

Keywords — Selflessness . . . Humanitarianism

Focus

A — *To know the pleasure of giving.*
B — *To love but not expect return.*
C — *To find the purity of expression.*

Characteristics

* Much interest in others
* Idealistic, often disappointed
* Romantic, loves with depth and passion
* Sensitive, sees the world with much feeling
* Creative with an active imagination

Positive factors

Universal love, brotherhood, charity, compassion, artistic genius, selfless service, philanthropy, humanitarianism, magnetism, sympathy, understanding, romance, generosity, the bird's eye view.

Negative factors
Emotionalism, egocentricity, sentimentality, dissipation of energies, impracticality, fickleness, dreaming.

Destructive factors
Dissipation, immorality, vulgarity, bitterness, moroseness.

Commentary
The Life Path 9 people find their reward in life by giving. They give of themselves, their love, their affection and their time. Their rewards for this are not obvious, yet this lesson can be the most rewarding of all. True love knows no cost, has no price, yet there is no reward greater than it.

Examples
Bette Davis, Orson Welles, Mae West, Guy De Maupassant, Carl Gustav Jung, Jacques Offenbach.

THE NUMBER 11

Keywords — Illumination ... Revelation

Focus
A   — *To be aware of the spiritual world.*
B   — *To combine the spiritual and the material.*
C   — *To recognise their channel of awareness.*

Characteristics
*   Very capable people

* Idealists with visions of a perfect world
* Dreamers with impractical fantasies
* Inspirational
* Much nervous tension

Positive factors

Intuition, revelation, invention, poetry, art, spirituality, fire, zeal, idealism, priestliness, evangelism, martyrdom, exhortation.

Negative factors

Aimlessness, shiftlessness, lack of understanding, fanaticism, superiority, imposition of the will.

Destructive factors

Miserliness, debauchery, degradation, dishonesty, devilry.

Note: see also destructives and negatives for Life Path 2.

Commentary

The Life Path 11 people are more dreamers than doers. Blessed with great capabilities they often spend their time in impractical daydreams. Often psychic they can be gifted with visions and perceptions that others do not understand. This might put them apart from the rest. Self sacrifice is not uncommon and the leaning towards martyrdom is quite apparent at times.

Examples

Harry Houdini, Richard Burton, Dr Benjamin Spock, John Glenn, Herbert C. Hoover, President Ronald Reagan.

THE NUMBER 22

Keywords — The Master Builder

Focus

A — *The mastery of internal forces.*
B — *The realisation of added awareness, perceptions.*
C — *The potential for great growth and development.*

Characteristics

* Extremely capable
* Practical, understands the problem
* Unorthodox, thinks across the problem
* Charismatic, the fire within them glows outwardly
* Nervous tension, an energy field buzzes below the surface

Positive factors

Power, idealism, practicality, direction, organisation, revitalisation, master of the material.

Negative factors

Get-rich-quick schemes, inferiority complex, grudging service.

Destructive factors

Viciousness, crime, black magic.
Note: see also destructives and negatives for Life Path 4.

Commentary

The Life Path 22 people have enormous potential, but most of their life is spent in trying to live with the energies within them. Consequently they seldom produce what they are ultimately capable of. The early years may be used either controlling the energies within them or trying to work some get-rich-quick scheme. Once they understand their potential then, with much will-power, they are able to direct it. Difficult to live with they find others cannot comprehend their energy, their drive, their need to achieve and accomplish.

Examples

Anton Dvorak, Oscar Petersen, Alistair Cook, Harold Wilson, Hugh Hefner, Henry Ford II.

THE BIRTHDAY NUMBERS

The First

People born on the 1st of the month are individualists with independent attitudes. They make good leaders, for they combine a good mind with executive ability. They have confidence in themselves, looking at things in a progressive, positive way. Usually ambitious, they plan on a practical and rational basis, often with an original approach. They are better at the broad strokes than the detail, and better at starting than continuing. The sometimes bluff external attitude hides a sensitive nature that is hurt deeply at times.

Examples

Dana Andrews, Robert Conrad, Tab Hunter, Dinah Shore, Walter Matthau, Debbie Reynolds, Queen Elizabeth I, E.M. Forster, J.D. Salinger, Lon Chaney, Jimmy Carter, Pat Boone, Edgar Rice Burroughs, Gary Player, Cardinal Cooke.

*

The Second

People born on the 2nd of the month fit in and work well with others. They prefer partnerships and co-operatives to going it alone. Sociable and friendly, they are diplomatic and would persuade rather than use any form of force. Affectionate, they have a great sensitivity to others' feelings, but are apt to lapse into some depressed moods. Good with details, they are better at continuing a project than starting a new one.

Examples

Desi Arnaz, Brian Aherne, Bing Crosby, Farrah Fawcett, Peter O'Toole, Bud Abbott, Groucho Marx, Marie Antoinette, Marquis De Sade, Isaac Asimov, James Joyce, Casanova, Havelock Ellis, Martha Washington, Jack Warner, Hedda Hopper, Mahatma Gandhi.

The Third

People born on the 3rd of the month are cheerful folk who express the joy of living. Good with words, they can excel at singing, speaking or writing. They may be in the entertainment industry, may sell, be writers or lecturers. They are creative with a good imagination. Friendly and sociable they can be enthusiastic and optimistic. Affectionate and loving, much feeling can cause some ups and downs. They tend to get involved with the trivial and superficial. Their interests are many but only at a surface depth, and as a result they get bored easily.

Examples

Mary Astor, Marion Davies, Jean Harlow, Paulette Goddard, Pierre Bonnard, Shelley Berman, Golda Meir, Rupert Brooke, Gore Vidal, Gertrude Stein, Thomas Wolfe, Alexander Graham Bell, Felix Mendelssohn, Doris Day.

*

The Fourth

People born on the 4th of the month are practical, rational and good organisers. They have the ability to manage things, be it in business or the home. They work long and hard with conscientious application to the task in hand. Self disciplined and responsible, they are patient, determined and persevering. Despite limitations they carry on but with stubbornness and rigidity. They show little affection thus do not attract much in return. Their feelings may be repressed, hiding their emotions. Their failing is that they concentrate on details and tend to miss the main event.

Examples

Jeff Bridges, Art Carney, Walter Cronkite, Deanna Durbin, Mitzi Gaynor, Audrey Hepburn, Gina Lollobrigida, Ida Lupino, Anthony Perkins, Eva Marie Saint, Buster Keaton,

Charles Lindberg, Elmer Bernstein, Louis Armstrong, Alice Cooper.

*

The Fifth

People born on the 5th of the month enjoy the company of others and work well in a group. They are talented, versatile and present new ideas well. Entertaining, amusing and enthusiastic, they make delightful companions. Socially their life can be a whirl, for they are much in demand. A quick, analytical mind makes them adaptable, but they are restless and the routine of life chafes at times. They may shirk responsibilities when it suits them.

Examples

Bette Davis, Robert Duvall, Samantha Eggar, Rex Harrison, Diane Keaton, Vivien Leigh, Elke Sommer, Spencer Tracy, Bob Newhart, Walter Mondale, Adlai Stevenson, Karl Marx, Guy De Maupassant, Pancho Villa, Otto Preminger, Art Garfunkel.

*

The Sixth

People born on the 6th have much interest in the home and family. Responsible, helpful and conscientious, they restore and maintain the harmony between others. They are sympathetic and kind with a good mind that understands and has empathy with others. Open, honest and generous, they can be a devoted spouse and parent who gives and receives affection freely. They are better at continuing than starting, and attend to those details others have overlooked. They have much emotion and sensitivity and are best with others who are equally as free with their feelings.

Examples

Lucille Ball, Sebastian Cabot, Sally Field, Zsa Zsa Gabor, Carole Lombard, Robert Mitchum, Sylvester Stallone, Mamie Van Doren, Raphael, Diego Velasquez, Andrei Gromyko, Achmed Sukarno, Marquis De Lafayette, John Paul Jones, John Philip Sousa.

*

The Seventh

People born on the 7th of the month usually have an interest in technical, scientific or spiritual matters. They have a fine mind that has a logical and rational approach to problems. Not too adaptable, they prefer to work on their own, yet they miss the company of others. Many have a wistful air about them; it seems they have difficulty in giving or receiving affection. Extremely sensitive, they are unable to communicate their deep emotions. Given to unusual approaches they often enjoy spiritual or psychic pursuits. They can be perfectionists and sticklers for detail.

Examples

June Allyson, Andy Devine, David Frost, Tom Jones, Anna Magnani, Darren McGavin, Anthony Quayle, Eli Wallach, Taylor Caldwell, Mata Hari, Madame Tussaud, Johannes Brahms, Joan Sutherland, Buddy Holly, Louis Prima, Ravi Shankar, Al Martino.

*

The Eighth

People born on the 8th of the month are self-confident and capable. Usually adept in the business world, their organisational, managerial and administrative skills enable them to handle large projects and money well. They seek material satisfaction from life. Practical and realistic, they tend to express little feeling. However, this careful reserve masks a deep well of emotion that they release in their own good time. They are better at starting than continuing, and better at the broad strokes than detail.

Examples
David Carradine, James Dean, Faye Emerson, Sonja Henie, Jack Lemmon, Yvette Mimieux, Mary Pickford, Silvia Sidney, Lana Turner, Esther Williams, Fernandel, Cyd Charisse, John Ruskin, Jules Verne, Anton Dvorak, Robert Schumann, Jean Sibelius.

*

The Ninth
People born on the 9th day of the month are humanists and sensitive to the needs of others. Broadminded, tolerant and compassionate they are much aware of others' feelings and sympathetic to another's plight. They express much emotion and are apt to find themselves in many dramatic situations. They give much in the way of friendship, affection and love, often without much obvious return.

Examples
Candice Bergen, Ward Bond, John Cassavetes, Lee J. Cobb, Ronald Colman, Kirk Douglas, Mia Farrow, Albert Finney, Cliff Robertson, William Fulbright, Sargent Shriver, Dean Rusk, Leo Tolstoy, John Milton, Joan Baez, Billy Joel, Les Paul.

*

The Tenth
People born on the 10th of the month are individualists with a compelling manner. They make good leaders, combining a good mind, a highly original approach and executive

ability. They have confidence in themselves, looking at things in a progressive, positive way. Often ambitious, they plan on a practical and rational basis. They may dominate a situation and have a strong will-power. They are better at the broad strokes than the detail, and better at starting than continuing. The sometimes bluff external attitude hides a sensitive nature that is hurt deeply at times.

Examples

Chuck Connors, Jimmy Durante, Barry Fitzgerald, Rhonda Fleming, Judy Garland, Helen Hayes, Paul Henreid, Sal Mineo, Norma Shearer, Max Von Sydow, James Whistler, Ray Bolger, Emily Dickinson, David O. Selznick, Dmitri Tiomkin, Giuseppe Verdi.

*

The Eleventh

People born on the 11th of the month may often inspire others by their example. They fit in and work well with others, sometimes to the point of being a martyr. They may be uncomfortable in the business world, preferring more spiritual pursuits. Sociable and friendly, they are diplomatic and prefer to persuade rather than force. Affectionate, they have a great sensitivity to the feelings of others. Nervous tension may cause depressions at times. They must find outlets for their high levels of emotion.

Examples

Yul Brynner, Eva Gabor, Pat O'Brien, Tex Ritter, Rod Taylor, Gene Wilder, Salvador Dali, Phil Silvers, King Farouk, Ferdinand Marcos, Fyodor Dostoevsky, D.H. Lawrence, Joseph Mankiewicz, Carlo Ponti, Hector Berlioz, Richard Strauss.

*

The Twelfth

People born on the 12th of the month are cheerful folk who express the joy of living. Good with words, they can excel at singing, speaking or writing. In business they have an original approach, but they might repress their feelings. They are creative with a good imagination. Friendly and sociable, they can be enthusiastic and optimistic. Very affectionate and loving, much feeling can cause many ups and downs. They tend to get involved with the trivial and scatter their energy. Their interests are many, but only at a limited depth.

Examples
Maurice Chevalier, Lorne Greene, Kim Hunter, Ann Miller, Jane Wyatt, John Singer Sargent, Milton Berle, John Bainbridge, Jack London, Florence Nightingale, Lily Pons, Connie Francis, Frank Sinatra, Tiny Tim, Charles Darwin, John Osborne

*

The Thirteenth

People born on the 13th of the month are practical, rational and good organisers. They have the ability to manage, be it in business or the home. However, they must try not to dominate others in the process. They work long and hard, are self-disciplined and responsible, patient, determined and persevering, and despite limitations they carry on. They can be stubborn, rigid, and may be dogmatic with others. They show little affection thus do not attract much in return. Their feelings may be repressed, hiding their emotions. Frustration and depression may get them down, for they are apt to feel restricted or limited in some way.

Examples
Lloyd Bridges, Harrison Ford, Howard Keel, Yves Montand, Kim Novak, George Segal, Robert Stack, Dick Van

Dyke, Cornel Wilde, Fidel Castro, F.W. Woolworth, Robert Louis Stevenson, Walt Whitman, Annie Oakley, Prince Aly Khan, Arnold Schoenberg.

*

The Fourteenth

People born on the 14th of the month enjoy the company of others. They are talented, versatile and present new ideas well. They are capable of hard work, but probably not consistently. They may have a tendency to over-indulge in eating, sensuality, alcohol or drugs. Restless and impatient, they can jump from one thing to another. A quick, analytical mind makes them adaptable and practical, but the routine of life chafes at times. They can often shirk their responsibilities.

Examples

Gene Barry, William Bendix, Brad Dillman, Howard Duff, Faye Dunaway, Lillian Gish, Brian Keith, Roger Moore, Dick Powell, Lee Remick, Thomas Gainsborough, Claud Monet, Terry Thomas, Pierre Salinger, William Penn, Prince Charles, Barbara Hutton.

*

The Fifteenth

People born on the 15th are interested in the home and family. Independent, responsible and helpful, they restore and maintain the harmony between others. Sympathetic and kind, with a good mind, they understand and have empathy with others. A devoted spouse and parent, they may repress their feelings somewhat. Better at continuing than starting, they attend to those details others miss. They have much love, are friendly and are appreciative of others.

Examples

Claire Bloom, James Mason, Margaret O'Brien, Cesar Romero, Saul Steinberg, Sir Walter Scott, J. Paul Getty, Agatha Christie, Algernon Charles Swinburne, P.G. Wodehouse, Harold Arlen, Gene Krupa, Melissa Manchester, Trini Lopez, Oscar Petersen.

*

The Sixteenth
People born on the 16th of the month are independent and on a different wave length. Maybe interested in spiritual matters, they have a fine mind that has a logical and rational approach to problems. Relatively inflexible, they prefer to work on their own yet they may feel isolated. Many have a wistful air about them, as they repress their emotions and have much difficulty in giving or receiving affection. Extremely sensitive, yet uncommunicative. Given to unusual approaches, they have potential for achievement. They can be perfectionists and sticklers for detail.

Examples

Ann Blyth, Charlie Chaplin, Noel Coward, Peter Falk, Henry Fonda, Ethel Merman, Suzanne Somers, Liv Ullmann, Peter Ustinov, Jerry Lewis, Nikita Krushchev, Jane Austen, George Santayana, Wilbur Wright, Eydie Gorme, Henry Mancini, Dusty Springfield.

*

The Seventeenth
People born on the 17th of the month are independent, self-confident and capable. Executive ability makes them adept in the business world, their organisation, managerial and administrative skills enabling them to handle large projects and money with ease. They seek material satisfaction from life,

practical and realistic, with an original approach. They express
little feeling and have difficulty in giving or receiving affection.
They are better at starting than continuing, and better at the
broad strokes than detail.

Examples
      Anne Bancroft, Diahann Carroll, James Garner, William
Holden, Rock Hudson, Dean Martin, Maureen O'Hara, Mae
West, Phyllis Diller, Hardy Amies, Benjamin Franklin, Davy
Crockett, Erskine Caldwell, Al Capone, Orville Wright, Arthur
Fiedler.

*

The Eighteenth
People born on the 18th are independent yet work well
with others. Idealists, sensitive to the needs of others, they are
humanists. Broadminded, tolerant and compassionate, they
have much will-power. In business they have executive ability
and organisational skills. Sensitive people, they express feelings
but much emotion is repressed. They are apt to find themselves
in many dramatic situations. They give friendship, affection and
love, often without much obvious return.

Examples
      Robert Donat, Greta Garbo, Betty Grable, Danny Kaye,
Melina Mercouri, Hayley Mills, Jack Palance, Robert Redford,
George C. Scott, John Travolta, Shelley Winters, Neville
Chamberlain, Pierre Trudeau, Roget, Andrew Segovia, Eugene
Ormandy.

*

The Nineteenth
People born on the 19th are in search of independence,
yet they are likely to find many obstacles in their path. They are

good leaders with a good mind and executive ability. They have difficulty in seeing themselves as others do. Self-confident, they look at things in a progressive, positive way. Ambitious with much will-power, they plan on a practical and rational basis. They are better at the broad strokes than the detail, and better at starting than continuing. A strong sensitivity can involve them in dramatic situations from time to time.

Examples

Ursula Andress, Jayne Mansfield, Lee Marvin, Dudley Moore, Merle Oberon, Hugh O'Brien, Cicely Tyson, Clifton Webb, Paul Cezanne, Leonid Brezhnev, Ogden Nash, Irving Wallace, Duchess of Windsor, Brooke Benton, Adelina Patti, Dolly Parton.

*

The Twentieth

People born on the 20th fit in and work very well with others. They prefer partnerships and co-operatives to going it alone. Sociable and friendly, they are diplomatic and would persuade rather than use any form of force. Very affectionate, they have an extreme sensitivity to others' feelings, but they are apt to lapse into depressed moods. Good with details, they are better at continuing a project than starting a new one.

Examples

Irene Dunne, Bo Derek, Errol Flynn, Bela Lugosi, Patricia Neal, Michael Redgrave, Diana Rigg, Dick Smothers, James Stewart, Gene Tierney, Natalie Wood, Henri Rousseau, Robert F. Kennedy, Adolf Hitler, Upton Sinclair, Jacques Offenbach.

*

The Twenty-first

People born on the 21st of the month are cheerful folk who express the joy of living. Good with words, they can excel at singing, speaking or writing. In business they have an original approach but they might repress their feelings. They are creative with a good imagination. Friendly and sociable, they can be enthusiastic and optimistic. Very affectionate and loving, much feeling can cause many ups and downs. They tend to get involved with the trivial and scatter their energy. Their interests are many, but only at a limited depth.

Examples

Jane Fonda, Goldie Hawn, Eleanor Powell, Telly Savalas, Zachary Scott, Ann Sheridan, Harpo Marx, Kurt Waldheim, Catherine the Great, Queen Elizabeth II, Benjamin Disraeli, Charlotte Bronte, Samuel Taylor Coleridge, Harold Robbins, Francoise Sagan.

*

The Twenty-second

People born on the 22nd of the month have a certain charisma and inner strength. Given much unusual perception and awareness they are capable of leading in new directions or of handling large-scale undertakings. Their unorthodox approach, responsibility and capability for hard work indicate their potential for creating new ventures in industry or business. They are idealistic and prefer to work for the good of all. However, if the energies become negative they could end up as master criminals.

Examples

Eddie Albert, Joan Fontaine, John Houseman, John Mills, Jack Nicholson, Ann Southern, Meryl Streep, Robert Vaughn, Charles De Gaulle, Edward M. Kennedy, Francis Bacon, John Dillinger, Claude Debussy, Werner Klemperer, Andre Kostelanetz.

The Twenty-third

People born on the 23rd of the month enjoy the company of others and work very well in a group. They are very talented, versatile and creative, presenting new ideas well. Sometimes a spokesman or peacemaker, they may be involved in many social activities. They love new experiences and travel and are much in demand. A quick, analytical mind makes them adaptable, but they are restless and the routine of life chafes somewhat. They may shirk responsibilities at times.

Examples

Janet Blair, Humphrey Bogart, Joan Collins, Joan Crawford, Gloria De Haven, Sandra Dee, Boris Karloff, Lee Majors, Mickey Rooney, Randolph Scott, Johnny Carson, Gene Kelly, George Frederick Handel, Sergei Prokovief, Bruce Springsteen.

*

The Twenty-fourth

People born on the 24th have much interest in the home and family. Responsible, helpful and conscientious, they restore and maintain harmony. They are sympathetic, kind and have empathy with others. Open, honest and generous, they can be a devoted spouse and parent who gives and receives love and affection, yet they may repress some feelings. They have a good mind and are creative, but are better at continuing than starting. Practical and rational, they are good organisers or managers and attend to those details others have overlooked.

Examples

Ernest Borgnine, Jackie Coogan, Ava Gardner, Phil Harris, Harry Houdini, Leslie Howard, Shirley MacLaine, Siobhan McKenna, Steve McQueen, Anthony Newley, Sidney Poitier, Barbara Streisand, Toulouse-Lautrec, Howard Hughes, Amelia Earhart.

The Twenty-fifth

People born on the 25th will probably be interested in the spiritual side of life. They have a fine mind that has a logical and rational approach to problems, but they are not too adaptable. Introspective, sometimes stubborn and self-centred, they prefer to work on their own. Many have a wistful air about them. They feel deeply but find it difficult to give or receive affection. Extremely sensitive, yet uncommunicative. Given to unusual approaches they often enjoy spiritual or psychic pursuits. They can be perfectionists and sticklers for detail.

Examples

Walter Brennan, Mel Ferrer, Van Johnson, Leonard Nimoy, Pablo Picasso, August Renoir, Raphael Soyer, Juliet Prowse, Georges Bizet, Enrico Caruso, Miles Davis, Ella Fitzgerald, Aretha Franklin, Elton John, Carly Simon, Tony Martin.

*

The Twenty-sixth

People born on the 26th are self-confident and capable. Usually adept in the business world, their organisational, managerial and administrative skills enable them to handle large projects and money well. They seek material satisfaction from life, are practical and realistic yet creative and artistic too. Sensitive beings, they express some of their feelings, are affectionate yet reserved. They are good at starting and continuing, and good at the broad strokes and the details.

Examples

Alan Arkin, James Arness, Sterling Hayden, Doris Lilly, Peter Lorre, George Raft, Tony Randall, John Wayne, Richard Widmark, Emlyn Williams, Honore Daumier, Jackie Gleason, Leon Trotsky, Aldous Huxley, George Bernard Shaw, Henry Miller, Tennessee Williams.

The Twenty-seventh

People born on the 27th are idealists, sensitive to the needs of others, and are humanists. They work well with others being broadminded, tolerant and compassionate. They have much empathy with and are sympathetic to another's plight. They express much emotion and are apt to find themselves in many dramatic situations. Sociable beings, they would use persuasion rather than force. They need to take time to rest and meditate. Sometimes self-centred or introspective, they give much in the way of friendship, affection and love, often without much obvious return.

Examples

Marlene Dietrich, Troy Donahue, David Janssen, Jack Klugman, Christopher Lee, Donna Reed, Gloria Swanson, Elizabeth Taylor, Franchot Tone, Tuesday Weld, Michael York, Henry Kissinger, John Steinbeck, Irwin Shaw, Wolfgang Amadeus Mozart

*

The Twenty-eighth

People born on the 28th are independent yet work well with others. They are good leaders, combining a good mind with executive ability. They have confidence in themselves, looking at things in a progressive, positive way. Often ambitious, they plan on a practical and rational basis, often with a creatively original approach. They are good at the broad strokes but capable with the detail. Diplomatic, they would use persuasion rather than force. Sensitive, they tend to repress their feelings.

Examples

Ann-Margret, Brigitte Bardot, Carroll Baker, Charles Boyer, Peter Finch, Ben Gazzara, Elsa Lanchester, Hope Lange, Marcello Mastroianni, Donald O'Connor, Artur Rubenstein,

Peter Duchin, Rudy Vallee, Lew Ayres, Sam Levene, Maggie Smith.

*

The Twenty-ninth

People born on the 29th of the month may often inspire others by their example. They fit in and work well with others, sometimes to the point of being a martyr. They may be uncomfortable in the business world, preferring more spiritual pursuits. Sociable and friendly, they are diplomatic and prefer to persuade rather than force. Affectionate, they have a great sensitivity to the feelings of others. Nervous tension may cause depressions at times; they must find outlets for their high levels of emotion. They give much in love, sometimes for a minimal return.

Examples

Warner Baxter, Gene Autry, Richard Attenborough, Ingrid Bergman, Dirk Bogarde, Richard Dreyfuss, Nelson Eddy, Anita Ekberg, Greer Garson, Trevor Howard, Beatrice Lillie, Barry Sullivan, Peter Paul Rubens, Rod McKuen, Frederick Delius, Anton Chekov.

*

The Thirtieth

People born on the 30th are cheerful folk who express the joy of living. Good with words, they can excel at singing, speaking or writing. They may be in the entertainment industry, may sell, be writers or lecturers. They are creative with a good imagination. Friendly and sociable, they can be enthusiastic and optimistic. Very affectionate and loving, much feeling can cause some ups and downs. They tend to get involved with the trivial and superficial. Their interests are many, but only at a limited depth, and as a result they get bored easily.

Examples

Eve Arden, Warren Beatty, Shirley Booth, Angie Dickinson, Gene Hackman, Susan Hayward, Fred MacMurray, Vanessa Redgrave, Vincent Van Gogh, Winston Churchill, Emily Bronte, Ezra Pound, Mark Twain, Lena Horne, Benny Goodman, Frankie Laine, Johnny Mathis.

*

The Thirty-first

People born on the 31st of the month are practical, rational and good organisers. They have the ability to manage, be it in business or the home. However, they must try not to dominate others in the process. They work long and hard, are self-disciplined and responsible. Patient, determined and persevering, despite limitations they carry on. They can be stubborn, rigid and may be dogmatic with others. They show little affection, thus do not attract much in return. Their feelings may be repressed, hiding their emotions. Frustration and depressions may get them down, for they are apt to feel restricted or limited in some way.

Examples

Fred Allen, Rex Allen, Tallulah Bankhead, Richard Basehart, Richard Chamberlain, Geraldine Chaplin, James Coburn, Dale Evans, Arthur Godfrey, Shirley Jones, Richard Kiley, Sarah Miles, Pola Negri, Jean Simmons, Ethel Waters, Henri Matisse, Eddie Cantor, Buddy Hackett, Chiang Kai-Shek, Zane Grey, John Keats, Norman Mailer, Mario Lanza, Franz Schubert.

*

THE PERSONALITY NUMBERS

The Number One

Keywords — Independent... Macho... Forceful... Dominant

Most likely you will be attracted by a Number One person's eyes, they are usually a dominant feature. Number One people will probably look you straight in the eye. They know what they want and they know how to get it. The forceful characteristics are in both sexes and they like to be on top. They love the limelight and an audience. They like nice clothes and can be very vain. They are good fathers and mothers, children seem always to be near. They tend to take things seriously but are generous to those they love.

Examples

Woody Allen, Glenn Ford, Andy Griffith, Hildegard, Judy Garland, Laurence Harvey, Yvonne De Carlo, Jimmy Durante, Mary Martin, Pamela Mason, George Peppard.

*

The Number Two

Keywords — Romantic... Passive... Gentle... Sentimental... Clinging

Number Two people are sentimental. They are always talking about the past and they never forget their first love. They love to be touched and caressed and always respond to a strong partner. They seem to prefer a dominant, overpowering partner to the more passive type. They make good friends and lovers and rather gentle parents.

Examples

Robert Ryan, William Powell, Rita Moreno, Peter O'Toole, Sally Kellerman, Eva Gabor, Jennifer Jones, Julie Harris, Cher, Bing Crosby, Brian Aherne.

The Number Three

Keywords — Ambition ... Argumentative ... Perfectionist

These people are the life and soul of the party. They are highly sexed and strongly motivated, friendly and very sociable. Good at conversation, but they argue too much. Sometimes heavy drinkers, which exaggerates their sexuality, their boasting and their arguments. A Three person tends to get his own way, so be warned.

Examples

Alan Ladd, Susan Hayward, Kim Hunter, Lorne Greene, Jane Fonda, George Hamilton, Deborah Kerr, Jack Lord, Wayne Newton, Virginia Mayo, Efram Zimbalist Jnr.

*

The Number Four

Keywords — Unconventional ... Stubborn ... Young at Heart

Number Four people can be highly sexual, fall in love with those younger than them and always be young at heart. They seem as if they know exactly what your problems are, giving out an air of understanding. Somehow they dress differently, they stand out in a crowd. They love the unusual, the different, and get bored with the same old routine. So unless you entertain them, watch out. They may find someone else different enough to make them move on!

Examples

Geraldine Chaplin, Walter Cronkite, Art Carney, Jeff Bridges, Sarah Bernhardt, Eva Marie Saint, Jane Russell, Lillian Russell, Ida Lupino, Dennis Weaver, Gig Young, Jane Wyman, Mitzi Gaynor, Carol Channing.

*

The Number Five

Keywords — Energetic . . . Lives a Double Life . . . Salesman

Number Five people like to create a good impression, no matter what the true facts are. Their love life is very complex, they are here now and gone tomorrow, possibly involved in two relationships at the same time. They can be very, very good or the extreme opposite. Their inner need for change and variety makes their life very hectic at times. Complicated people, they rarely stand still long enough for you to weigh them up.

Examples
Lillian Gish, Vivian Leigh, Diane Keaton, William Bendix, Janet Blair, Brad Dillman, Howard Duff, Sandra Dee, Joan Collins, Bette Davis, Gene Barry.

*

The Number Six

Keywords — Security . . . Luxury . . . Affection . . . Romance

Number Six people are sexy and alluring, their movements are sensual. There is a fullness about them and you will be conscious of their chest or breasts. Once well acquainted, however, their life-style may become too routine for many partners. Their need for a loving security can mar the spontaneity and freedom that others may need in a relationship. They love luxury, but this tends toward a rather restrictive life-style.

Examples
Penny Marshall, Robert Mitchum, Ed McMahon, Cesar Romero, Lilli Palmer, Loretta Young, Rudolph Valentino, Walter Huston, Stewart Granger, Phil Harris, Zsa Zsa Gabor, Ava Gardner, Petula Clark, Sebastian Cabot, Claire Bloom.

*

The Number Seven

Keywords — Mystic . . . Restless . . . Spiritual

Number Seven people are hard to understand, sometimes moody or in a dream, they seldom seem to be on your wavelength. They may find alcohol gives them problems at times, preferring the spirit in a bottle to the spirit in people. Maybe melancholic, they have an affinity with the Piscean image. The feet are important. These are spiritual people and life can be difficult for them.

Examples

Ann Blyth, Buster Crabbe, Andy Devine, June Allyson, Anthony Quayle, Barbara Stanwyck, Eli Wallach, Sonny Tufts, Walter Winchell, Peter Ustinov, Liv Ullmann, Ethel Merman, Anna Magnani, Peter Lawford, Noel Coward.

*

The Number Eight

Keywords — Conservative . . . Fatalist . . . Old Fashioned

Number Eight people are cool and calm on the outside and a time bomb on the inside. It just requires someone to set the detonator and in their good time they will become a ball of fire. They are fatalists by nature, old-fashioned with conservative ideas. However, do not let that fool you. When they let go — watch out. All that reserve and constraint only builds the power within them, they just need the right catalyst — could that be you?

Examples

Lynn Redgrave, Paul Newman, Yvette Mimieux, Julie London, Al Jolson, Dustin Hoffman, Sonja Henie, Sterling Hayden, Jose Ferrer, James Dean.

*

The Number Nine

Keywords — Argumentative ... Leaders ... Love attention

Number Nine people are highly sexed, love attention and do not mind how they get it. They seem to like some sense of danger in their love-life. Travellers, loners, philosophers, they like to be looked up to. Not for them the time and place of the number Eight. They are spontaneous, the here, the now and wherever. They love a debate or an argument, especially if the family are around. Forceful in their lovemaking, they may have a few scars to tell the tale.

Examples

Broderick Crawford, Candice Bergen, Ward Bond, Beau Bridges, Kirk Douglas, Lee J. Cobb, Hedy Lamarr, Kathryn Grayson, Glenda Jackson, Hayley Mills, Robert Redford, Donna Reed, John Travolta, Susannah York, Tuesday Weld, Franchot Tone, Gloria Swanson, Vincent Price, Melina Mercouri.

*

THE EXPRESSION NUMBERS

The Number One

Keywords — Independent ... Ambitious ... Original ... Creative

People with an expression number 1 have administrative capabilities. Born with executive potential, they are independent and ambitious. When expressing their positive face they are ambitious, positive and self-confident. With much will-power they prefer to follow their own course than follow one set out by another. They have a good mind and the drive to make it work for their advancement. When showing their negative side, however, they are likely to be dominant and bossy whilst also egotistical and stubborn. Likely to be self-centred and selfish, they can be lazy and dependent on others. They must recognise their latent potential and not be deterred by undermining influences.

*

The Number Two

Keywords — Co-operative . . . Sensitive . . . Skilful . . . Adaptable

People with an expression number 2 probably prefer to be in a partnership or a co-operative rather than going it alone. In the past they may have found others have got the credit for their ideas. They are diplomatic in handling complicated and touchy situations. Skilful at handling groups, they implement their ideas by persuasion rather than force. When showing their positive face they are friendly, modest, tactful and courteous. However, they can be shy and uncertain, if not timid and fearful. This leads to apathy and indifference. They have to recognise that their over-sensitivity leaves them open to imaginary slights, their ego suffering in the process.

*

The Number Three

Keywords — Expressive . . . Creative . . . Communicative

People with an expression number 3 have a talent with words, they communicate well. They may find teaching, selling, acting or demonstrating rewarding vocations. When expressing their positives they are a pleasure to be with, they have optimism and enthusiasm. Friendly, affectionate and loving, they express the joy of living. They are very social, combining happiness with grace and charm. They love a good time and can inspire others. The negative face causes them to scatter their forces and become trivial and superficial. Inclined to gossip they may be critical and moody or just too easy-going. They must try to identify their latent artistic talent and float out that joy within them.

The Number Four

Keywords — Practical... Hard Worker... Faithful...
Sincere

People with an expression number 4 are good managers, they
organise well. They have a practical down-to-earth approach to
things, with an ability to bring plans to a practical format. They
are able to work long and hard and are conscientious and
dependable. When expressing their positive side they are
serious, sincere, honest and faithful. They fulfill their obligations
and proceed with the job despite limitations. They are helpful,
patient, persevering and determined. Frustrations and the
feeling of limitation may cause them to express their negative
face. They may be dominant and bossy or an excessive
disciplinarian. They can be rigid, stubborn and dogmatic with a
fixed approach. They must realise that their concentration on
the detail causes them to lose sight of the overall picture. They
must try to see the forest and not just the trees.

*

The Number Five

Keywords — Talented... Loves Change... Progressive...
Clever

People with an expression number 5 are capable of doing
almost anything they try, and usually very well too. Clever and
analytical, they are good at presenting ideas; they know how to
approach others to get what they want. Good at selling, they
have a built-in ability to find the best route to close the sale.
They enjoy working with people and are entertaining and
amusing. When expressing their positive side they are enthusiastic, adaptable and progressive. They love change and like to
travel. Their negative face causes them to be restless and
impatient, likely to scatter their energy or prone to over-
indulgence. They may loose sight of the objective by being
sidetracked by some new interest or flame.

The Number Six

Keywords — Responsible... Helpful... Comforting... Sympathetic

People with an expression number 6 are helpful and conscientious. Capable of balancing inharmonious situations, they excel in the care of others, they give comfort and help to those in need. When expressing their positive side they are loving, friendly and appreciative. Usually involved in some domestic activity, they make a good spouse and parent. The negative face can cause them to be too exacting of themselves, even to the extent of being a doormat to others. Sometimes they are unable to separate helpfulness and interference. They often worry and become too anxious, or find themselves unable to express their individuality.

*

The Number Seven

Keywords — Analysis... Philosophy... Discriminating

People with an expression number 7 search for the truth of things. They have a good mind that enables them to become an authority on matters. Interested in the scientific, technical or spiritual areas of life, they delve beneath the surface to discover hidden truths. When expressing their positive face they are very logical and rational but show little emotion. Too much emotion can cause them much distress. They are difficult to get to know because they seem to operate differently. Their negative side makes them introspective and not very adaptable. They may be critical and unsympathetic, and would prefer to work on their own. They have not much trust in others and tend to be perfectionists.

*

The Number Eight

Keywords — Executive . . . Ambitious . . . Efficient . . . Realistic

People with an expression number 8 have managerial capabilities and administrative skills. They are good with their judgement of both money and people. They excel in the material world. A realistic, practical approach enables them to handle large projects and interests. They are very capable of running their own business. Their positive face shows an ambitious person with energy and self-confidence. Their negative side makes them stubborn, rigid and over-ambitious, impatient to proceed. They are very exacting of themselves and others.

*

The Number Nine

Keywords — Humanistic . . . Philanthropic . . . Sensitive

People with an expression number 9 work well with others and are very sensitive to others' needs. They have an ability to inspire others and may be teachers, religious leaders or counsellors. They are humanistic and give of themselves. Their positive face shows a person with much understanding and selflessness. They are idealistic and have much personal ambition. Their negative side can make them selfish and unaware of their own true feelings. They can become insensitive to the needs of others. They may be detached and uninvolved, yet wanting much friendship and love.

*

The Number Eleven

Keywords — Inspirational . . . Sensitive . . . Capable . . . Dreamer

People with an expression number 11 have much inner strength and often inspire others with their example. They are very aware and sensitive, with a good intuition. They have an ability to see into the spiritual world, giving a depth and perspective to the material world they see around them. When expressing their positive face they are idealistic and capable of any work they undertake. They are apt to be deeply involved with art, music and beauty. Their negative face can get them lost in daydreams, sometimes becoming quite aimless and without direction. They have much nervous tension and may be temperamental. They are apt to be impractical, often inflicting unrealistic ideas and standards on others. They may wish to impose their ideas without consideration of the other's feelings.

*

The Number Twenty-two

Keywords — Master Builder ... Leader ... Innovator ... Eccentric

People with the expression number 22 are very capable at whatever work they choose. They have the ability to excel in the material world. They have much unusual perception and an awareness of non-material forces. They have charisma, their inner strength being very evident. Their positive face shows an idealist with a practical approach. They may often work for the good of all. Their negative side can display much inner tension, with the tendency to be selfish and dominating. Their inferiority complexes may make it impossible for them to harness the power that runs within them. There can be a tendency to get involved with get-rich-quick schemes.

*

THE SOUL URGE NUMBERS

The Number One

Keywords — Independence . . . Attainment . . . Self Identity

People with a soul urge 1 have an inner need to be as independent as possible. They wish to be able to act on their own. They aspire to being the leader, free to start or pioneer any venture they choose. They prefer to take a strong domineering role rather than be submissive to another. They want to be a success in a large enterprise, to prove their individual worth. They would prefer to be concerned only with the broader strokes, leaving the detail to others. They would rather keep their own opinions, preferring not to seek another's advice.

*

The Number Two

Keywords — Relationships . . . Co-operation

People with a soul urge 2 have a primary inner need for friendship, affection and love. They would rather be married than single. They desire to work with others as a team rather than to be out there on their own. They seek sensitive, warm and genial people like themselves.

*

The Number Three

Keywords — Expression . . . Communication . . . Joy

People with a soul urge 3 wish to express their inner joy of living. They want to join in on social events, to be with people. They have many gifts, and will express their artistic talents in as many ways as they can. They wish their home and environment to reflect the beauty and joy they see in life.

The Number Four

Keywords — System . . . Limitation . . . Organisation

People with a soul urge 4 have an inner need for a stable, ordered life. They wish an ordered approach to life and do not like too much change. They want to be involved in solid, conventional, well-organised activities. They are prepared to work hard for what they have, willing to serve others diligently.

*

The Number Five

Keywords — Freedom . . . Excitement . . . Travel . . . Pacemaker

People with a soul urge 5 have an inner need to be free and to do those things that make life for them worth living. They want travel, romance, adventure — anything to make them feel alive, to know that their life has not been wasted. They hate being governed by limitations of any kind and tend to reject the standard values and traditions.

*

The Number Six

Keywords — Security . . . Balance . . . Responsibility . . . Love

People with a soul urge 6 have an inner need to give love and affection. They are responsible and would like to feel that they are good parents and spouses. They want to take on the reins of responsibility, to feel that they are needed and loved. They love children and need a family of their own to care for.

*

The Number Seven

Keywords — Spirituality ... Understanding ... Wisdom ... Truth

People with a soul urge 7 have an inner need to retreat from the world. They need to retreat from the outer world to develop their resources and find themselves. They wish to learn the inner truths to gain wisdom and understanding. If they had the choice they would avoid the world of business. They prefer contemplation and study to activity and adventure.

*

The Number Eight

Keywords — Success ... Power ... Wealth ... Status ... Satisfaction

People with a soul urge 8 wish success and power from life. They have an inner need to excel in business or industry. They wish status and recognition from their fellows. They probably have considerable material needs to satisfy, as they may feel bound to attempt to live to a lifestyle that is commensurate with their ambitions.

*

The Number Nine

Keywords — Giving ... Sympathetic ... Humanitarian ... Kind

People with a soul urge 9 wish to give of themselves to others. They have an inner need to feel that they have been of service to others. They would be sympathetic and kind, with much empathy for another's situation. Sensitive people, they possess a deep understanding of life and its problems. Idealists with strong motivations, they would contribute much to make this world a better place to live in.

The Number Eleven

Keywords — Idealist ... Dreamer ... Spiritual ... Intuitive

People with a soul urge 11 have a tendency to become dreamers. Often of a religious or spiritual nature their dreams take on Utopian proportions. They have much inner strength when they devote it to a particular cause. They have a good mind but are often very selective in their choice of companions. Much nervous tension is brought on by high levels of awareness.

*

The Number Twenty-two

Keywords — Awareness ... Ambition ... Idealist ... Leadership

People with a soul urge 22 have an inner need to contribute their abilities in some constructive venture to aid mankind. A high intelligence enables them to envisage vast undertakings for the betterment of all. High levels of nervous tension are brought on by their extraordinary powers of awareness and perception. They can fall into the trap of becoming too dominating in the pursuit of their ideals.

*

THE KARMIC NUMBERS

The Number Thirteen

Keywords — Limitation and Order

The Focus

The Karmic Number 13 is focused on people's application to work and achievement. These people are likely to find themselves boxed in on all sides, and their approach becomes rigid and dogmatic as they feel limited and restricted. Eventually they rationalise their position; but not until they understand that the cause is within themselves do they fully come to terms with it.

The Lifepath Debt

These people will find their opportunities very limited. No matter what they do they always seem to be constrained and limited in some way. It is their unbending, rigid attitudes that cause their own restrictions.

The Expression Debt

These people will work very hard, usually in a one-track direction. It is their dogged persistence that limits their vision and thus negates the overall achievement.

The Soul Urge Debt

These people are discontent with the restrictions their workload place on them. Constantly looking for new directions, whatever they try is marked by little satisfaction upon completion.

*

The Number Fourteen

Keywords — The Use of Freedom

The Focus

The Karmic Number 14 is focused on people's constructive use of freedom. They will be like a rolling stone that gathers no moss, moving from one thing to another. They will over-indulge in eating, sensuality, excitement, alcohol or drugs. Not until they curb their excessive appetites and make good use of the time given them will they rationalise their position; however, only when they fully understand that the cause is within themselves will they come to terms with it.

The Lifepath Debt

These people must learn the lesson of change. They must learn to appreciate the moment of now, to know the wonder of full bloom. They must not be disappointed when it dies. Until they reach this point they will find sadness at every turn.

The Expression Debt

These people will have a very hazy idea of their own talents. They will probably be disappointed with their work. They constantly need to regroup their forces in order to move on.

The Soul Urge Debt

Important relationships can be interrupted by delays and separation. Until they recognise the cause within, they will continue to be impatient and emotionally irresponsible.

*

The Number Sixteen

Keywords — Analysis and Understanding

The Focus

The Karmic Number 16 is focused on people's relationships to others. They tend to be cold, aloof and distant people, somehow different and difficult to know. They are probably selfish, self-centred and introspective. Their development is at their whim, and as a result they become more and more isolated. Their marriages and close relationships can be difficult to maintain. Until they develop a selfless, loving attitude their problems will continue to magnify.

The Lifepath Debt

These people will learn the transient nature of reality. This impermanence will be felt in those areas dearest to the heart. They think they have achieved something — then — it is gone! Their love-life can shift abruptly, other things ending quite suddenly.

The Expression Debt

These people can find that they have unintentionally tripped themselves up in some way so that their work is affected. Or some unexpected thing will cause them to lose what they have worked for. They must not rely on their material status too heavily.

The Soul Urge Debt

Their choice of friends may be a little wanting, or they may find people they would trust are suddenly unreliable. Close friends cease to be, due to some unforeseen happening.

*

The Number Nineteen

Keywords — Independence and Individuality

The Focus

The Karmic Number 19 is focused on people's opinion of themselves. They are either totally self-centred, cannot see others' needs and are always surprised at others' opinions of them, or they are completely dependent on others and resentful about it. Both their selfishness and their inability to stand on their own two feet are brought about by internal forces. Not until they fully understand that the cause is within themselves do they come to terms with life.

The Lifepath Debt

These people will find that their ego is the cause of their downfall. The self-centred attitude limits their view, and their positive actions are undone only by their own selfishness. Often they are exposed as the dominating, selfish people they are.

The Expression Debt
Their dominating approach may turn others off, so that they never get the recognition they deserve.

The Soul Urge Debt
These people will be unable to hide their self-centred ways. Their own self-interest will be exposed and will be their own undoing.

THE PYTHAGORAS PLANES

The Plane of Thought

Example — a person born 12th March, 1967

Sometimes known as the plane of the planner, this number combination gives a unique blend of intellect, intuition and expression. Such people have an inherent appreciation of method and order. Planning things out, the organisation of a business or the efficient running of a household are natural expressions of the Plane of Thought.

Tidiness is a prime factor with these people, but they do not always carry out their own instructions. As a result they may find themselves involved in some arguments concerning their lazy inclinations. They have an ability with words, they express their thoughts clearly and they may be superior speakers or debaters. Paradoxically, in their early years they could have experienced a problem expressing themselves. In such cases the children should be shown outlets for their creative abilities, otherwise moodiness and an introverted nature could well result.

Examples
Margaret Thatcher, born 13.10.1925, has the Plane of Thought and also the Plane of Purpose. She is an excellent case study of these dynamic, positive number planes in action. Eight Presidents of the United States of America had the Plane of

Thought in their chart. Also Jean Simmons, Alan Arkin, James Arness, Richard Attenborough, Carroll Baker, Brigitte Bardot, Anne Baxter, Bill Bixby, Humphrey Bogart, Marlon Brando.

The Plane of Dexterity

Example – a person born 4th February, 1967

The definition of dexterity is that of being either manually or mentally clever. Thus it is often the mark of the lateral thinker, the person who can think across a problem.

It may also indicate one who has a wonderful ability with the hands. A good example of both of these characteristics combined in one individual is Sir Winston Churchill, politician, soldier, statesman and, in his later years, artist.

The person with the line of dexterity may have hated schoolwork as a child and as a result would have been labelled as being a bad scholar. It is reported that both Churchill and Einstein suffered this lot. Albert Einstein also had the line of dexterity in his birthchart.

Generally these people are healthy with a good reserve of stamina. They are probably attracted to out-of-doors pursuits. If not then they need to find an outlet for these bubbling reserves of creativity. Playing a musical instrument may prove to be the answer. Often these people, if not involved in some creative pursuit, may be overly concerned with worldly desires. They may find themselves totally caught up in the material side of life.

Examples

Albert Schweitzer, Thomas Edison, Walter Brennan, Polly Bergen, Geraldine Chaplin, James Garner, Jack Klugman, George Murphy, Walter Winchell, Sylvester Stallone, Donald Sutherland, Gina Lollobrigida, Harrison Ford, Einstein and Churchill (as above).

The Plane of Empathy

Example — a person born 8th September, 1963

The Plane of Empathy in the chart indicates an innate understanding of others. This most beneficial factor enables people to project themselves into another's situation, thereby to understand and to have compassion. This Plane also indicates a high level of intellect and the potential of a very good memory. However it can also be a sign of someone who is quite lazy.

These people have a preference for things intellectual, sometimes to the extent of ignoring others' feelings. On the other hand, when they want to express emotion they are more than capable. These are thoughtful people, but when a crisis threatens they tend to overlook the feelings of others, not because of any innate callousness, but simply because they become so absorbed with the problem at hand.

As children they do not do very well at school, not for any lack of ability, but simply because they get bored with the highly structured educational system. The temptation to fool around becomes just too great. Once away from the disciplines of the system they will work hard to make a success of their lives.

Examples
Harold Wilson, Glenda Jackson, Richie Benaud, Johnny Cash, Roy Emerson, James Arness, Stewart Granger, Sterling Hayden and Al Jolson.

The Plane of Tenacity

Example — a person born 4th May, 1968

The Plane of Tenacity in the chart indicates a resolute persistence to get the job done.

Everyone born this century with this plane in their chart will also have the Plane of Purpose or Determination, giving them the drive and spirit to keep on, even though all seems to be lost. This characteristic stubbornness often leads them to success.

Sometimes known as the Plane of the Will, the people with this plane have much will-power and are intent on following their own course of action. The combination of the '4', the '5' and the '6' makes for a strong, balanced character, loyal and faithful, a true friend. However, these people can be difficult to handle, but with patience and understanding the rewards are well worth the effort. From children they express themselves by deeds of kindness, but this intensity sometimes leaves them unable to see another's point of view. Their need for personal involvement is so great that they may be accused of being disinterested in others. Acute stubbornness can be a failing, all too often they will dig their heels in.

Examples
Oscar Wilde, Diane Keaton, Michelangelo, Raelene Boyle, Gregory Peck and Jack Dempsey were all born with the Plane of Tenacity in their chart.

The Plane of Passion

Example — a person born 2nd May, 1968

The Plane of Passion in a chart lends an ardour and intensity to all that these people do. This awareness makes them very serious about whatever they undertake. Everyone born this century with this plane also has the Plane of Purpose in their chart, lending determination to their efforts. Whatever they do, they do with conviction, with purpose. There is nothing half-hearted about them. Highly sensitive, they recognise another's happiness or sadness in an instant. For this reason complete strangers are often attracted to them, unburdening their cares with ease. The strong characteristics of the person with the Plane of Passion always seem to carry the day.

People with this Plane often devote their lives to a principle, sometimes leaving home and family in some distress as there is a tendency to concentrate solely on the task in hand. As a result they are often accused of being inconsiderate to others. They must learn to consider others more, or else they themselves will suffer.

One cause of considerable distress can be their emotional involvements. Their intensity and passion is seldom matched by others, leaving a frustration and an emptiness that is hard to reconcile.

A high proportion of writers have this Plane in their chart.

Examples

Pablo Picasso, Dr Carl Jung, Lord Nelson, Florence Nightingale, Isadora Duncan, Somerset Maugham, Sinclair Lewis, Archibald Macleish, Frances Parkinson Keyes, Havelock Ellis, Rainer Maria Rilke, Hans Christian Anderson, Virginia Woolf, William Faulkner, Stephen Birmingham, Ralph Waldo Emerson, George Bernard Shaw.

The Plane of Energy

Example — a person born 7th February, 1968

The Plane of Energy endows people with tremendous reserves of power. They have to be on the go all the time.

Sometimes called the Plane of Action, there is action a-plenty with these people. As children this can be a source of never-ending frustration for the parents, if they do not realise the needs of their offspring. These children must be physically active or involved in some project all the time, or hyperactivity could well result. An indication of the frustrations caused by inactivity could be the outbreak of allergies. As children, early to bed and early to rise must be the rule, and as adults they would be well advised to remember those lessons so well learnt as children.

Throughout their life diet will play a significant part. It is important that they take great care over what they eat, and in the way that they spend their lives. They are not suited to city life; the noise, the traffic and the pollution can all contribute to stress levels. Suppressed nervous energy can cause any number of illnesses. But when they overcome these hazards in their daily existence, they will be power houses of energy and action. They can literally move mountains in the achievement of their goals.

Examples

Albert Einstein, Edgar Rice Burroughs, Shirley Bassey, George Plimpton, Amelia Earhart, Percy Bysshe Shelley, Dennis Wheatley, Walter Winchell and Nelson Rockefeller.

The Plane of Insight

Example — a person born 7th May, 1930

The Plane of Insight in the chart gives people singular powers of perception. From children they would have stored images and impressions; when older, they finally put the jigsaw together. As time passed they adapted these observations of their surroundings into a greater knowledge of their fellow man.

If born this century, people with the Plane of Insight in the chart will also have the Plane of Purpose. Thus they are doubly endowed with both compassion and determination. Life is not kind to them, probably because they have been given the inner strength to deal with all manner of troubles. As a result they have a calmness and serenity that marks them apart from the rest of us.

A shrewd mental ability is inherent with this Plane, and suitable vocations are those where this excellent reasoning power can best be put to work. An appreciation of music is likely, harmony and balance being second nature to such people.

A spiritual awareness is common with them. Maybe this is the cause of that calm and peace in their demeanour.

Examples

John Keats, Diahann Carroll, Anne Baxter, Elton John, Cilla Black, Zane Grey, William Turner.

The Plane of Purpose

Example — a person born 2nd May, 1970

The Plane of Purpose in a chart indicates a high level of determination. These people are endowed with the will to get the job done. They plan their activity and carry on till the end, no matter what. Their purpose in applying themselves to the task is a keynote of their attitude to life.

Anyone born this century with a '5' in their birthdate has the Plane of Purpose in their chart. As the '5' is a power number it is not surprising that this century has seen by far the greatest growth and development. This is a plane of strength and once the person has identified with his aim he will carry on until the end, never to give up. If the person has more than a single '1' in their chart they are likely to be more stubborn. With more than one '5' they are likely to be more intense. Or if they have more than one '9' they are probably more intelligent but much harder to live with.

Examples

John Keats, J.F. Kennedy, Frank Sinatra, Rod Stewart, Mel Torme, Herbert Von Karajan, Dmitri Shostakovich, Dietrich Fischer-Dieskau and Martin Luther King were all born with the Plane of Purpose in their chart.

The Plane of Sensitivity

Example — a person born 1st March, 1970

The Plane of Sensitivity in a chart is an indicator of a very caring, loving spirit. These people have a very loving nature and would do all for the ones that they love, but they have been given a hurdle in life that they must overcome — their sensitivity. As children they were probably very shy with an inability to express their emotion.

As they have grown older they would have learnt ways to bypass this problem, sometimes by retiring and sometimes by aggression. However, unless they have learnt to address the problem directly it will still exist. This inability to express emotion may have left them with a label that they were cold and heartless. The plain fact was that they were neither: they were simply incapable of letting their true feelings be known.

They have to learn the way to let their inner deep emotions out, to find the way to float out their love on the ocean. If they do not it will be bottled up and could lead to serious illness. In the end it is up to them. They have the problem. They also have the cure. It is only a question of recognising it.

As children, they should never be admonished in front of others. Take them to one side and talk to them quietly, give them your love and you will be so richly rewarded. If they retire to nurse their wounds in private, seek them out. Talk to them, show them that you care. Never let that resentment build up within them for it can be so very, very destructive. These are very loving people. Give them love so that they may give theirs back.

Examples

David Frost, Helen Hayes, Susan Hayward, Rita Hayworth, Tab Hunter, David Niven, Ethel Merman, Anthony Quayle, Irene Ryan, Robert Ryan, Dinah Shore, Loretta Young, Gig Young, Efram Zimbalist Jnr all were born with the Plane of Sensitivity in their chart.

The Plane of Saturn

Example — a person born 7th July, 1900

The Plane of Saturn in a chart indicates that these people will probably experience great frustrations during their life. Although this Plane of missing numbers is a signifier of a difficult life, it also shows that the bearer has a great inner strength to undertake these trials. Very often people born with this missing number combination bring upon themselves their own trials, either by impulsiveness, impatience or that demon that seems to lurk within all of us at times. With the person born under the Plane of Saturn, you can be sure that they will pay the price for their misdemeanors. However, they have the fortitude and strength to weather the storm.

Sometimes the cause of their problems is that they expect too much from life, and become disappointed when it does not measure up to their high standards. This could be because, as children, they had been spoilt by their overcaring parents, and when the harsh realities of life confronted them they were very much unprepared. They may expect too much from others and were not themselves prepared to give much in return. Whatever the cause, they need much love and affection if they are not to feel victimised in the process.

As children they may exhibit various complaints from allergies to simply lethargy, to more serious illnesses. These are all symptomatic of the one cause — a sense of victimisation, a sense of being hard done by. It is up to the parents to be neither too soft nor too hard, but to give their children what they need most — love. That love is not to be confused with a new bicycle or a new game to play. These people need to identify with the realities of life to know that they alone have not been singled out for some special treatment.

Examples

Jean Simmons, Roger Smith, Barry Sullivan, Pamela Mason, Donna Reed, Robert Redford, Michael Redgrave, Silvia Sidney, Douglas Fairbanks Jnr, all had the Plane of Saturn in their chart.

The Plane of Vision

Example — a person born 2nd April, 1980

The Plane of Vision in a chart indicates a paradox, a person with a great gift of vision and foresight, yet who can be an extreme skeptic.

Whereas these people can be very religious, their concepts of other than orthodox spiritual entities can be very inhibited, and yet they have the capability to envisage vast and complex schemes. Their limitation to the spiritual is a barrier or hurdle placed in their way. They can find great solace in the arts, for here in two- and three-dimensional form they can see the beauty of things. It is the intangible, the unproven, the mystic that they find so difficult to accept.

They frequently suffer from eyestrain, headaches, some-times migraine. They must take time to rest, they must retire every now and then to regather their bearings, to re-establish their relationships to things.

Children with this Plane can be very moody, they are expressing their skepticism in moodiness. They are unable to accept the world as they find it, need much kindness, love and understanding. They need parents who are in tune with them and help them to see the world as the rich and wonderful place it can be. They need to be taught to enjoy life and the world that they live in.

Examples

Clifton Webb, Eddie Albert, Dana Andrews, Chuck Connors, Charlie Chaplin, Farrah Fawcett, Peter Finch, Ava Gardner, Judy Garland, Paul Henreid, Julie London, Susannah York, all had the Plane of Vision in their chart.

The Plane of Dedication

Example — a person born 3rd April, 2005

No one born in the last three hundred years has had the Plane of Dedication in their chart. As the year 2000 rapidly approaches, this free number plane demonstrates the dramatic changes in the world's population profile. It is but another factor of the new age of mankind that commences with the turn of the Century.

The Plane of Inspiration

Example — a person born 1st May, 1887

People born with the Plane of Inspiration in their chart are likely to have brilliant flashes of inspired thought. Freed from the '9' and the '3', these people probably experience moments of true clarity. Some call this Plane the Plane of Poor Memory. From the examples below, it would not seem to fit too well! Nobody born since 1888 has had this Plane in their chart. The year 2000 sees their arrival on earth again. Truly an indicator of change.

Examples

Quincy Adams, John Logie Baird, Sarah Bernhardt, Georges Bizet, Billie Burke, Lord Byron, Casanova, Raymond Chandler, Frederick Chopin, Samuel Taylor Coleridge, Isadora Duncan, Dame Edith Evans, Samuel Goldwyn.

The Plane of Perception

Example — a person born 9th March, 2005

No one born this millennium can have the Plane of Perception in their chart. As the year 2000 rapidly approaches, this free number plane dramatically demonstrates how near we are to a new age of mankind. What will these people be like? It is difficult to say, for as near as we are we are not of their time. What is clear is that a new age of mankind is dawning soon.

The Plane of Development

Example — a person born 3rd June, 2007

No one born this millennium can have the Plane of Development in their chart. As the year 2000 rapidly approaches, this free number plane dramatically demonstrates how near we are to a new age of mankind. What will these people be like? It is difficult to say, for as near as we are we are not of their time. What is clear is that a new age of mankind is dawning soon.

THE PYTHAGORAS NUMBERS

The Number 1

The Single 1 in the Chart

Example — a person born 8th February, 1956

People born with a single 1 in the chart have a problem expressing the deep emotions. Considerable frustration can build up because they are unable to express what is troubling them. Sometimes they are not even aware of the problem itself, they just feel troubled and ill at ease. They have to learn to get it all out, to say what they feel, to release it all. If not they will tend towards introversion and occupations that limit personal communication.

Two 1s in the Chart

Example — a person born 1st February, 1964

People born with two 1s in their chart have no problem in expressing their feelings, in fact they are conscious of a need to do so. The drive for individuation is healthy and not unbalanced. As a child they probably yelled or cried when upset or angry. They do not need to learn the art of self-expression.

Three 1s in the Chart

Example — a person born 16th March, 1951

People born with three 1s in the chart have the problem of over-communication, yet paradoxically they do not say what they feel. They may chatter on about something but seldom achieve any depth to their conversation. Very often they find release for the inner emotions by writing, whether it be just a diary or more ambitious literary goals.

Four 1s in the Chart

Example — a person born 11th April, 1951

People born with four 1s in the chart can be somewhat overbearing at times. This is because they experience great difficulty in expressing their deeper emotions, their self-esteem suffering in the process. They may attempt to dominate in a conversation rather than communicate, so try to get them to see your point of view as well.

The Number 2

The Single 2 in the Chart

Example — a person born 8th February, 1976

People born with a single 2 in their chart are sensitive and intuitive. When meeting people for the first time they are able to form an opinion about someone instantly and they are rarely wrong. Their sensitivity can leave them somewhat at the mercy of life if they do not learn to control their deeper emotions.

Two 2s in the Chart

Example — a person born 2nd February, 1974

People born with two 2s in their chart have the ability not only to form an instant opinion of someone, but also to know what it is the other person is feeling or thinking.

This wonderful power, though, can be misused, for these people have a special talent for getting their own way. This is a marvellous gift and a good percentage of these people will find a vocation in the church or social work. However, if the power is used for selfish ends it can result in skin-deep, clandestine relationships and unhappiness.

Three 2s in the Chart

Example — a person born 23rd December, 1962

People born with three 2s in the chart will have a very highly tuned sense about other people. In their early years this can literally mean that they are swamped with information pouring in on all channels. This can leave them in a confused state and it is not unlikely that they will be unable to control themselves, and violent outbursts of temper could be expected. On the other hand they may attempt to close themselves off from the world. Whatever, this over-sensitivity may lead at times to some antisocial behaviour. These people need kindness and under-standing, for they have intuitive powers that are quite unique.

Four 2s in the Chart

Example — a person born 12th February, 1922

As with the person with three 2s in the chart, a person with four 2s is the same but more so. Louis Pasteur was a person with four 2s in his chart. Obviously he found a way to use the heightened sense of awareness and power that this number combination gives. Family and friends need to be aware that this is a very special person with a unique and wonderful gift.

The Number 3

The Single 3 in the Chart

Example — a person born 3rd February, 1956

People born with a single 3 in their chart have the gift of a logical mind that thinks things through. Accordingly these people are often creative, having the power to conceive large projects. Their reasoning ability is good and the complexities of abstract thought are not lost to them.

Two 3s in the Chart

Example — a person born 3rd February, 1903

People born with two 3s in their chart have a heightened reasoning ability. They will always think things through before they start anything. They may be classed as non-conformists but this is not out of any need to be different. It is just that they have been able to perceive the best route to the end result, and if it does not conform, so what! They could well be in administration or some organisational profession.

Three 3s in the Chart

Example — a person born 23rd December, 1933

People born with three 3s in the chart have strong mental abilities that should be balanced by some form of physical outlet. There is a tendency to become totally absorbed in their own thoughts, and like as not they dream a lot. They can be multi-talented, and because of the optimism of the three influence may find themselves attracted to show business. There is a danger of them becoming too wrapped up in their own thoughts, so try to make them see your point of view as well.

Four 3s in the Chart

Example — a person born 13th March, 1933

People with four 3s in their chart have heightened mental activity to the extent that they can become totally absorbed in their own thoughts. This has the inevitable result of making them very self-centred. The tendency for dreaming may become a habit, therefore it is vital that these people balance the extremes of mental activity with some form of physical activity, sport, athletics, swimming, etc. This is a very powerful number combination. It has great potential if developed correctly, but little can be achieved if you are up in the clouds all the time.

The Number 4

The Single 4 in the Chart

Example — a person born 3rd April, 1956

People born with a single 4 in their chart are practical, down-to-earth people. They tend to be perfectionists and, when young, need to be encouraged otherwise they may never be satisfied with what they achieve. A talent with the hands is indicated here, so an aptitude for music and the playing of an instrument is a possibility.

Two 4s in the Chart

Example — a person born 4th February, 1974

People born with two 4s in their chart have a heightened ability with the hands — carpentry, pottery, sculpture, music, etc., are all areas where these people could excel. There are great organisational skills here also and the desire to take a task from beginning right through to the end. Tidiness and neatness is of prime significance to them.

Three 4s in the Chart

Example — a person born 24th April, 1964

People born with three 4s in the chart have great ability with the hands and the arts. However, as wonderful as these talents are the increased potential of the 4 energy heightens their fixed approach to life. They can be quite rigid in their approach to life and with such inflexibility may be very hard to get along with. They should find a highly physical outlet to balance the mental energies.

Four 4s in the Chart

Example — a person born 4th April, 1944

This is a very rare combination and the comments that apply to three 4s are more heightened here. It is vital that these people release their energies in some form of highly physical but creative outlet. Otherwise confusion and great frustration can result.

The Number 5

The Single 5 in the Chart

Example — a person born 5th April, 1976

People born with a single 5 in their chart have been given the gift of intensity, whether it be determination, passion or ardour, it is theirs. They have the power to influence others, to convince others. However as good as this gift is, there are drawbacks, and they are not the easiest of people to live with. They need freedom, freedom to act and freedom to think.

Two 5s in the Chart

Example — a person born 5th February, 1975

People born with two 5s in their chart have great emotional intensity. In fact their determination and passion are such that at times it can overbalance them. Their strong character traits enable them to influence others with ease. However, this only makes them harder to handle, their domestic life suffering in the process.

Three 5s in the Chart

Example — a person born 25th May, 1957

People born with three 5s in the chart have so much intensity and power that they find dangerous outlets to release their drive. It goes without saying that this can be, and is, extremely hazardous. The lesson in life for these people is self control. Once mastered, the world is at their bidding. They have the power, they have the mastery. Their only challenge is themselves.

Four 5s in the Chart

Example — a person born 5th May, 1955

This is a very rare number combination and with it goes a rare challenge indeed. As the person with three 5s has power, so the person with four 5s is power personified. There are only three days in a century when these people can be born, and as a result there are relatively few examples of them. The attraction to danger is probably their largest hazard for nowhere else are they liable to find the challenges to satisfy them. Consequently they are at the mercy of fate. As with three 5s, self-control is their challenge.

The Number 6

The Single 6 in the Chart

Example — a person born 6th March, 1973

People born with a single 6 in their chart have a great love of the home. They thrive on harmonious surroundings and become anxious in stressful situations. They are happy when they are able to please the people they love. They are suited to bear the responsibilities of family life. Their ability to maintain a good rapport with their loved ones makes them excellent parents or guardians.

Two 6s in the Chart

Example — a person born 6th February, 1965

People born with two 6s in their chart seem to lack confidence. This may have been caused by over-protective parents. As a result they have probably tended to lean too heavily on their parents, leaving themselves weaker in the process. Otherwise the problem may have stemmed from tension and strife within the home environment. They have to learn the lesson of self-reliance and independence.

Three 6s in the Chart

Example — a person born 26th June, 1956

People born with three 6s in their birthdate can be highly creative, so much so that they need much understanding from their loved ones. Art or music can be satisfactory release valves for this great internal energy and sensitivity. They may have to apply spartan levels of self-control when dealing with their offspring; the tendency to become over-protective is very real.

They must realise that children have to grow up and move away from the home environment, and it is the parents' responsibility to equip their children in all aspects of life, including freedom.

Four 6s in the Chart

Example — a person born 6th June, 1966

This is a very rare number combination as it occurs only three times a century. These people have extreme levels of sensitivity and creativity. As a result great emotional problems can result if they do not find a satisfactory outlet for their inner drives. They must apply great self-control when dealing with their loved ones, especially children. The tendency to be over-protective is very marked. This number combination can indicate severe emotional hardships if the individual does not come to grips with the great energies within him.

The Number 7

The Single 7 in the Chart

Example — a person born 5th April, 1976

People with a single 7 in their chart are thinkers or philosophers. When life's problems strike them they want to know the reason why. They wish to learn from their trials. Many feel that this number signifies hardships of one kind or another. It may. However, people with a 7 in their birthchart will not make light of it, they will learn from their experience.

Two 7s in the Chart

Example — a person born 5th February, 1977

People with two 7s in their chart have great inner strength to handle life's challenges. This number combination indicates the need to delve under the surface of things and to understand the very forces that cause us to do and to be what we are. It gives a distinct leaning toward understanding the spiritual and motivational side of life.

Three 7s in the Chart

Example — a person born 27th July, 1975

People born with three 7s in the chart have great inner strength, and will probably need it. These people go right to the core of things, to understand the universe and the nature of life. Very often psychic or prophetic, they attune naturally to the spiritual and the religious. They can be quite remarkable. Their mission in life they alone understand, however, it is most important that they do not allow life's problems to undermine that magnificent fortitude they have been born with.

Four 7s in the Chart

Example — a person born 7th July, 1977

This is a very rare number combination, and people with it have all the strength of the three 7s plus. They have the Plane of

Saturn in their chart, so life for them will not be an easy affair.
Such spirituality as is inherent in the combination of four 7s in
the birthchart will aid them immensely in their struggle, and
perhaps they might take time to show the rest of us the way?
Most probably psychic and prophetic, the potential for some
form of self-sacrifice is quite pronounced.

The Number 8

The Single 8 in the Chart

Example — a person born 5th April, 1978

People born with a single 8 in their chart have the ability to be
extremely tidy and methodical, with an aptitude for accurate
assessment. This method and order is a measure of the positive
qualities of the '8'. However, if life gets on top of them they are
likely to show the negative traits of the 8, which is a tendency to
become very restless, and possibly 'A rolling stone that gathers
no moss.' They have to exert self-control when things get
tough.

Two 8s in the Chart

Example — a person born 8th February, 1981

People born with two 8s in their chart have a sharpened sense of assessment which can make them either very successful or very unsettled, maybe at times both. In public they are likely to be very proper and self-controlled, but off-duty they are demonstrative and full of life. Their control of finances is excellent. As children they probably saved their money well, whilst as adults they make very wise and sound investments. They hate to sit back and remain idle. They never wish to let the grass grow under their feet.

Three 8s in the Chart

Example — a person born 8th August, 1958

People with three 8s in the chart have heightened powers of assessment; however, much of their early years could be spent in a very unsettled way. They have to come to grips with this energy within them and to realise that this life is not pointless or aimless. Once their energy is properly harnessed they have great potential to show the rest of us the way. Jules Verne had three 8s in his chart, a better example of someone with great wisdom and vision is hard to find.

Four 8s in the Chart

Example — a person born 28th August, 1988

This is a very rare number combination and the energy of the 8 is dominant. As with the three 8s, these people need to realise life's potential and to control their wanderlust tendencies. That they have the potential there is no doubt. Their powers of assessment are excellent. An example of the vision of someone with four 8s is John Logie Baird, the inventor of the television.

The Number 9

The Single 9 in the Chart

Example — a person born 1st March, 1948

Everyone born this century has at least one 9 in their chart. The single 9 therefore does not have any individual significance to us. However, the single 9 represents the ability to express emotion without fear. The 9 is the number of intellect, a signifier of intelligence. It is the number of humanity, of aspiration, of idealism. Does not this century, as distinct from the last century, demonstrate the power of the 9 in the evolution of Man on this planet?

Two 9s in the Chart

Example — a person born 4th February, 1979

People with two 9s in their chart have a heightened awareness of idealism and ambition. So much so, that they can sometimes be accused of being quite exclusive in their choice of companions, for if someone does not measure up to their intellectual requirements they may well be avoided. The deep-thinking ability of the double 9 is a great gift, but remember also that tolerance is a virtue.

Three 9s in the Chart

Example — a person born 29th September, 1976

People born with three 9s in the chart have exceptional powers of idealism and ambition. This great mental activity can lead them off into their own world at times, to become lost to reality. It also can cause great mental frustrations which will lead to frightening outbursts of temper. These outbursts can be quite unbalancing, so these people need to find some outlet for their heightened internal energies. They also need to guard against being too selective and discriminating in their companions. Properly harnessed this energy is a powerhouse for the good of all; uncontrolled, it can be very destructive.

Four 9s in the Chart

Example — a person born 9th September, 1949

This is a very rare number combination that has all the characteristics of the three 9s with perhaps even more emphasis on a tremendous activity of the mind. As for the three 9s, this mental activity needs to be offset by some physical exercise or activity. The energy must be controlled or else, these people can become very unbalanced. Temper outbursts may be common, but this must be viewed as an outlet of great frustrations. These outbursts should be directed into some physical activity as a release valve.

THE PYTHAGORAS NUMBERS — THE MISSING NUMBERS

The Missing Number One

Example — a person born 3rd September, 2004

No-one born in the present millennium can have the number 1 missing from the chart. The 1 is the natural vehicle to express a person's individuality. These children of the 21st century will need to find other avenues to express their natures, to demonstrate their uniqueness. As the year 2000 rapidly approaches, this missing number demonstrates how near we are to a new age of mankind.

The Missing Number Two

Example — a person born 1st May, 1984

People born with a 2 missing from their chart need to develop their intuition about others. This missing number indicates a lack of sensitivity when young. They may develop this ability as they grow old, time is a great teacher. However, for the meantime they should take great care when selecting their companions, otherwise they could be in for some rude shocks.

The Missing Number Three

Example — a person born 6th July, 1920

People born with the number 3 missing from their chart tend to see only the solid and the tangible. They have trouble perceiving abstract concepts, consequently their early attitudes to art and beauty can be limited. They need to develop this awareness to fully appreciate the beauty and joy that life holds in store for them.

The Missing Number Four

Example — a person born 1st May, 1980

People born with the number 4 missing from their chart probably led a life of chaos until they realised that they needed a system to live by. The missing 4 indicates a lack of order and system in day-to-day life. Most people as they grow up develop this skill in one way or another, but these people need to work that little bit harder to find it.

The Missing Number Five

Example — a person born 6th July, 1920

The number 5 is the number of power. People with the 5 missing can lack drive in their early years. They need to develop an inner discipline to see them through the rigours of life. We all need determination to finish a task, but these people need to develop an experience of accomplishment to enable them to continue to the end. As children they should be given many incentives to let them feel the power of their achievements.

The Missing Number Six

Example — a person born 1st May, 1980

People with the number 6 missing from the chart may have experienced a difficulty in communication with at least one parent. Maybe the parent was missing completely, or they may have sensed a disunity between the parents. Whatever the cause, a sense of alienation or a frigid family background can give these people an early hurdle in life to overcome.

The Missing Number Seven

Example — a person born 6th August, 1920

People born with the number 7 missing from the chart lack the number of inner fortitude. In their early years they could have been overly shy and reluctant to put themselves forward. They have to develop an awareness of the spiritual side of life, to realise that we learn from our mistakes.

The Missing Number Eight

Example — a person born 1st May, 1970

People born with the number 8 missing from the chart have to learn to look before they leap, to resist the impulsive and the rash. They hate monotony and tedious tasks. Not too good with money, they have probably learnt to their cost the penalties of extravagance and of not watching the budget.

The Missing Number Nine

Example — a person born 6th February, 1887

People born with the number 9 missing from the chart have a fear of expressing their emotions. A lack of understanding for their fellows is implicit in this missing number. They have to develop an awareness of others, cultivate a desire to know their brothers. They should avoid any tendencies to hide themselves away from life. They must learn not to isolate themselves and their emotions.

CYCLES OF TIME

Chapter 15

A Small Discovery

He thought he saw an Albatross
    That fluttered round the lamp:
He looked again and found it was
    A penny-postage stamp.
'You'd best be getting home', he said
    'The nights are very damp'.

Lewis Carroll

A Coincidence?

Coincidences happen in all manner of ways. Fate has some strange disguises in his travelling bag. During the writing of this book a coincidence occurred that had a direct bearing on both the structure and the substance of the product you are now reading: a coincidence that had a direct bearing on cycles, astrology and numerology. In fact it could be viewed as an object lesson, an example of 'Acausal Synchronicity', Jungian style.

The agony and the ecstasy of writing a book is hard to describe. Sometimes the process is all consuming, enthralling and compelling, other moments are much less than this. Sometimes it is just a determined and relentless plod towards the end. An end that always seems to be just as far away as when you started.

An Eleven Year Cycle?

One Sunday morning, during one of these relentless periods, I was patiently typing out the interpretations of the Pythagoras Cross. Gradually advancing through the numbers — single 1, two 1s, three 1s, four 1s, single 2, two 2s etc., etc. (I had in fact started this section a day or so earlier.) I continued — single 3, two 3s, three 3s, four 3s. At each example I would give a date that contained the correct numerals for the number combination I was describing. Four 3s? Well, the date had to be in March of 1933. I realised that the next four 4s would have to be in April of 1944, eleven years later on. Moreover, as I described each case of multiple numbers, I was aware that each time I was describing an accentuation of the characteristics of the base number. In other words, four 3s are the accentuation of the three characteristics; four 4s the accentuation of the four characteristics, etc.

Now, as I tell the story, this seems so blatantly obvious but until that point I had had no reason to investigate this factor. It suddenly dawned on me that here was a cycle: every 11 years, 1 month and 1 day there would be an accentuation of the characteristics of the next number in the series. Musing about this for a while, I wondered if I could find any correlation or corroboration in astrology for this 'new' cycle I had discovered.

Investigation

Moving quickly to the bookcase, I took down the ephemeris. An ephemeris is a book the astrologers use to plot the birthchart. It lists all the planet positions for each day. I looked at the ephemeris for the period 1931 to 1980. The starting date then would have to be the 3rd March 1933. I noted down all the planetary positions for that day. Moving on I noted all the positions for the 4th April, 1944, and so on for 1955, 1966 and 1977.

Gathering all my results I scanned them to see if I could see any similarities. Looking at the outer planets, Mars through Pluto, I could see no similarities at all, they all seemed quite random, just as one would expect. However, when I studied the inferior planets Mercury and Venus, it was a very different matter. Mercury had a definite pattern on the dates that I had chosen and Venus also showed some apparent pattern.

This was fascinating. Was there a connection? Had I found something?

Now enthused, I prepared an individual chart for each of

the twenty dates that I had the planetary positions for. Each individual chart was so designed that it gave both a numerological analysis of the birthdate, and the planetary data for that day, the eventual objective being to compare the numerological characteristics with an astrological chart for each date.

Mercury and Venus?

In due course I completed each one of the twenty pages. Hurriedly I scanned the results. Yes! There definitely was a correspondence between the dates of accentuation and the positions of Mercury and Venus. In each case Mercury was rising, some 16 to 20 degrees ahead of the Sun, and in each case Venus was setting between 10 and 50 degrees behind the Sun.

I was excited. I studied all my astrology manuals to find a guide, a clue, but there was nothing. I could not find anything that described this phenomenon or anything like this phenomenon. I studied the astrological symbolism of Mercury and Venus to discover some forgotten facet that would lead to an understanding of this happening. There was nothing. I contacted my astrology teacher to see if she had any idea about these results. However, other than being interested, she could not offer any rational explanation for the effect.

There seemed to be no answer to the puzzle, yet here was the evidence. Here was correspondence between the orbits of Mercury and Venus and these dates of accentuated numerological characteristics. For some days I mulled over what I had discovered. What did it all mean? What was really behind it all?

A Cosmic Red Herring?

Then one day, looking at the result for the 999th time, I noted that there was a much closer correspondence between some days than others, the days that were most out of line being the 30th and 31st of March, 1933. The pattern for 1933 had already been confused because Mercury had turned retrograde in the middle of the month, thus I had discounted those results somewhat. However, on closer examination there seemed to be little reason for these days at the end of the month to be so much out of line with the rest.

At that moment a flash of the cold light of truth entered my brain. I quickly checked the sidereal period of Mercury. The sidereal period is the time Mercury takes to make a complete orbit of the Sun, to arrive back exactly where it started. The sidereal period was 88 days. I then calculated how many days there were in 11 years 1 month and 1 day, allowing 2 days extra for leap years. The answer — 4048 days. I divided 4048 by 88 — the answer was exactly 46. No wonder Mercury's position was so close each 11 years. It had made precisely 46 orbits of the sun each time, so as to arrive at exactly the same relationships with the Sun each eleven years.

On the 30th and 31st March, 1933, Mercury had moved considerably from where it had been in the middle of the month. It was this fact that had given me the clue to the answer.

But what of Venus? Its sidereal period was 224.7 days. Divided into 4948 this gave 18.015, close enough for one to see that there was correspondence. Close enough to fool one!

The mathematics of the exercise were over, the answer was clear. It was simply a mathematical coincidence, a mathematical coincidence that had turned into a cosmic red herring!

Some Questions to be Asked!

However on reflection there were questions raised by this exercise that demanded answers.

Question 1

Does Astrology support Numerology?

Traditionally the answer has always been found by the subjective appraisal of a specific individual. Now this was quite different. What I had stumbled upon was a group, defined by dates, that supposedly by numerological standards had quite definitive characteristics. Could this numerology case-study be supported by astrology? A study of each case came up with the same answer. There did not seem to be any common or obvious corroboration between astrology and the attributes clearly demonstrated by numerology.

Answer — No!

Question — Why Not?

Conclusion — It seems we have to ask astrology questions on its own terms of reference. Go beyond these boundaries and astrology does not work.

Question 2
Does the Sun sign support Numerology?

Presuming the numerology to be correct, on the relevant dates, did the Sun's position in the Zodiac support the numerological traits of the 3, the 4, the 5, etc.?

Answer — No!

Question — Why Not?

Conclusion — Sun sign characteristics are broad and general. Everyone does not have to fit into an identical mould.

Question 3
Is the sidereal position of a planet to the Sun significant?

If Mercury was always rising and Venus always setting, why did astrology not support this? The answer is plain. The thing was only a mathematical coincidence — or was it? Should astrology not support this finding?

Answer — It does not!

Question — Why not?

Conclusion — As for question 1, astrology is not structured to be accessed in this way. Astrology has not evolved this way.

The simple fact of the matter was that these dates that I had selected demonstrated quite clearly a numerological group of characteristics that could not be supported by astrology as a group.

If you were to take a specific individual, born on any one of these dates, if you took his birth time, his place of birth, calculated his astrological natal chart, you would find that astrology would provide a clear analysis of the man's character. However, in this numerological group, astrology did not work. Here now was a situation where a group of numerology characteristics could not be supported, in a general sense, by astrology. Why?

Beyond a Coincidence!

I had not set out with this objective in mind but with what I supposed to be a cycle and for that matter still could be a cycle. I had also found this set of case studies that went right to the roots of the matter.

Now the bells of Jungian acausal synchronicity were peeling out in my brain. This thing had gone far beyond the bounds of normal coincidence yet that was all it was, coincidence. During the writing of a book I had accidentally come across obscure planetary statistics that corresponded to human characteristics, that correspondence eventually proving to be a mathematical coincidence. However, that coincidence was to provide the very evidence to prove the theory of the book. The thing had taken on a very different dimension now. The coincidence itself seemed to offer its own proof!

The Summary
The answers now were to me quite plain.

One: the sidereal periods of planets are functions of the cycles of time. They exhibit a harmonic relationship to these cycles. It is as Pythagoras states: 'Number is the law of the universe.'

Two: the period of eleven years between examples of accentuated personality characteristics was a cycle, it had to be. Did not both Mercury and Venus exhibit a close harmonic relationship to it? Hence the close correspondence on all of the dates analysed.

Three: the exercise demonstrated that numerological characteristics could be supported by planetary motion.

Four: Mercury's retrograde motion in March 1933 caused significant errors. This demonstrated that the traditional methods of astrology were wrong. Planetary motion must be evaluated on an actual three-dimensional basis with the Sun at the centre, not the Earth-centred two-dimensional system that has been handed down to us.

Five: the fact that astrology could not support the findings demonstrated the specific manner in which man has structured the science to access information.

Six: astrology works because man has made it work. The stars are but a giant time-map in the sky. Man's ingenuity has enabled him to adapt the sidereal times of the planets to relate to the Cycles of Time.

Seven: because man has had only a limited number of planets, with a limited number of sidereal periods, man's knowledge of these time-cycles is very narrow.

Eight: as a result of this limited knowledge, astrology can fit only where it touches. Try other time cycles with it and it will not work.

Nine: Astrology has outstripped the mythology that created it; it is hemmed in by narrow barriers of its own creation.

Ten: the mechanics of astrology are obscure, complicated, difficult. Why is this so? It is because man in his invention has had to adapt his calculations to fit the star map in the sky. That is why there is such complication, such complexity to astrology. It is that adaptation that causes the dilemma of astrology.

Eleven: the Cycles of Time are the common denominator. They are the linking factor. It is they that connect astrology and numerology together. It is they that by their repetitive nature permit predictions of the future.

Chapter 16

A Different Point of View

In the dawn of the Aquarian Age
In this time of bountiful technology
When all the world is a television stage
Why then this interest in astrology?

When computers daily run our lives
When drugs or child abuse are no surprise
When man goes to the Moon and survives
Why search the heavens for that infinite prize?

6,000 years of Astrology

By now you must have come to the conclusion that
there is much more than your own personal opinion to assert
that astrology works. Astrology may not be the oldest profession
on earth but it certainly comes very close to it. The evidence
speaks for itself. If something did not work it would not last six
years let alone 6,000. Think of it. For 6,000 years man has
studied, practised and developed astrology. Yet we still do not
know what it is that makes astrology work. However, the
evidence is there, the heritage of 6,000 years leaves no doubt —
astrology works.

Let us take a hard look at this question of why astrology
works, but before we do it is necessary that, for the moment
anyway, we unlearn something.

Forget Planetary Influence

For a moment put away those concepts of planetary
influence. Put aside those words from the past that tell us it is the
planets that cause us to be what we are, and do what we do.

The truth of the matter is, as we have seen throughout the
book, no-one knows and nobody can tell us what causes
astrology to work.

Planets or Cycles?

Of all the champions of astrology, Michel Gauquelin must go to the head of the list. What an incredibly determined Frenchman he turned out to be. But what was it that he was searching for? Why — proof of, or proof for, astrology. And he found it!

But he also found a cycle or cycles — the diurnal motion of a planet is nothing but a cycle. Gauquelin had his sights set on establishing astrology — nothing else, the blinkers were firmly in place. Hence my point in the chapter 'The Neo Astrologers'. If Gauquelin had wanted to disprove astrology he might have recognised what he found as a cycle.

It is my contention that cycles are not just any random length. They are of a determinate duration, that duration determined by the structure of the universe. Hence all the evidence Mr Dewey has accumulated on cycles. It is my contention that the sidereal period, the diurnal motion and many other natural events are all symptomatic of the one entity — The Cycles of Time.

These comments are not meant in any way to detract from Michel and Francoise Gauquelin's achievements. What they achieved is not in question. The question is — was it astrology they proved or Cycles?

Astrology is the Study of Cycles

Once you look at this issue from the perspective of cycles the thing takes on a very different aspect. Let me quote a current, world-famous, modern astrologer — Alan Oken: 'Astrology is the study of cycles. More specifically, astrology focuses upon the relationships which exist between the larger cycles of the Earth and the personal cycles of the individual.' (*Alan Oken's Complete Astrology* p. 517)

I am sure that Alan Oken did not place the interpretation that I place on his words. However, looked at from the perspective of cycles the thing takes on new meaning. What I wish to point out is that we are already aware of these cycles but we have not looked at them from a realistic perspective. Because by tradition we have been taught to look at these effects as being some planetary influence, some force or control coming from the stars, we are blind to other possibilities.

Planetary Influence is Inbred

Remove the blinkers put on us by tradition and the thing suddenly takes a different form. The assumptions no longer seem so valid. We have lived so long with this idea that the planets influence us, that it has become inbred.

As an example, listen to what Christopher McIntosh has to say about 'A New Science of the Stars', from his book *Astrology* p. 86: 'We may yet see the development of a new science that is halfway between astrology and astronomy.'

The presumption is that the new science must be in our concept of three-dimensional space. I maintain it is not, it is in the Ouspensky concepts of the 4th, 5th and 6th dimensions. In other words, in time.

Cycles are Footprints

Let me give an analogy of what these cycles are.

Imagine for a moment you are on a walk in the country. Rounding a clump of bushes you come upon a flat slab of rock. The slab has lain for millions of years and there in the centre is the footprint of what must have been a dinosaur. You have never seen the animal, it died millions of years before you were born, yet you know it has been where you are standing. You do not know what it looked like but you do know it was very, very big. You do not know how heavy it was but you know it was very heavy. Last and most important, you know that *it existed*.

That is what these cycles are. They are footprints of some force, energy, influence. Call them what you like, one thing is sure. They control and if they do not control, they most certainly influence. Walk on the beach at low tide. You do not have to be told where the high tide was, the sea has left its evidence, its footprint in the sand. Cycles are the solid evidence of trends, they are the visible proof to the pattern of things. They reveal the existence of some energy, force or influence.

Planets Do Not Control Us

One would not deny that both Sun and Moon exert gravitational influence on us. The evidence has already been presented in this book but the idea that the outer planets exert a control on us is, I believe, quite specious.

However, if one said that the planets in their orbits demonstrate an influence then that is another matter. Put another way, if one sees a cork bobbing in a pond, one does not assume it is the cork that is doing the work. One knows that there are unseen currents making it bob up and down. Just so with the planets. If the planets are in synchronism with events on earth, it is because the whole Solar System responds to unseen forces — those forces being the currents of the Cycles of Time.

Taking this concept one step further one might say that a planet's motion, the time periods of its rotation, were in synchronism with the fundamental forces of the universe, thus in synchronism with those forces that cause us to be what we are. In other words, the footprints of the planets are in time with the footprints of our life. A concept very much in line with Mr Dewey's findings. The footprints of cycles are in our records, they are in our statistics. It is time we recognised that, instead of talking mumbo jumbo about planetary influence.

Cycles are Predictable

From the evidence presented there can be no doubt that these cycles exist or, I should say, continue to exist. They are operating whilst you are reading this book — *right now*. You will not be aware of them but in a few months or few years time they will be a matter of record, another set of statistics, another set of footprints. We can say then that we see, afterwards, this influence or footprint in our records and statistics.

'Cycles show us that this influence is both mechanistic and

repetitive ': to quote Lester C. Thurow, Professor of Management and Economics, Massachusetts Institute of Technology.

'If one could find cyclical regularities, the analyst could go beyond descriptions of the past and make predictions about the future. History would come alive as a predictive science.'

A Different Point of View

Cycles and the Intangible

Astrology deals with the intangible, with our emotions, aspects of character, our fate or fortune. Cycles, on the other hand, are statistics that deal with the tangible. Even so that tangible entity can still represent the intangible in such things as church attendance or the incidence of mob violence.

The reason for cycles not showing more of the intangible is, I submit, simply due to the fact that we are not able to collect this data. In other words, there is no reason to suppose that Cycles do not show aspects of personality or aspects of our fate. In fact there is evidence to suggest that they do. Take the case of church attendance as an example. We saw in the statistics church attendance went in cycles. It follows that the group emotions that caused those attendances also went into the same cycle. The one is symptomatic of the other. Rationally, it is obvious that there are cycles of emotions. For further proof any marriage guidance counsellor will attest to the seven year cycle in marriages. Is that not a cycle of emotions?

Let us now see what we can glean from the strange coincidence that I experienced in the chapter 'A Small Discovery'. Was the thing I experienced so much of a coincidence? Let's take another look.

In the first place, I was searching for confirmation of what I thought was a cycle of heightened characteristics. I found a correspondence in the orbit of Mercury and a close correspondence in the orbit of Venus. Was that an incredible coincidence? On second thoughts probably not. What I found was that the orbit of Mercury was the 46th harmonic of the time cycle I was searching for. I suspect that what I found was no more than the ancients found when they searched the heavens for correspondence with events on earth. I found a correlation between aspects of personality and the orbits of Mercury and Venus. Astrology could not show me that correlation because astrology was never programmed to answer questions of that nature. However, the fact remains that such a correlation exists. There is a correlation; no matter how much you consider it coincidence, there is a correlation between this cycle of heightened characteristics and the movements of the planets. That much I have shown. We can say then that there is a correlation between cycles and aspects of personality.

One might argue that the correlation I discovered is not one that the main body of astrology recognises. I would agree but I would make the point that neither was the discovery of the Gauquelins. Not that I wish to compare my little discovery with that of the Gauquelins. I do not. I merely wish to establish the similarity. I wish to establish the correlation between cycles, the movement of planets and aspects of personality. I submit that these results show such a correlation does exist.

Astrology and the Planets

The tradition of the centuries makes it inevitable that there is considerable complication to the study of astrology so it would be as well if we condensed that complication to a simple expression: astrology is the study of the ten bodies of the solar system as they move around the ecliptic or zodiac. It is the study of the relationships of these bodies to their position in the zodiac and their angular relationship to each other.

The ten bodies that the astrologer takes note of are the Sun, Moon and the eight remaining planets. Any astrology manual will tell you that a sign, a 30 degree span of the Zodiac, is relatively inert until a planet moves into it. In other words, it is the planets that are the functioning entities, not anything else! Thus it is the motion of the planets and little else that determines astrology.

The Planetary Clock

Now as we know, each planet revolves around the Sun, and the path it takes is called the ecliptic. Because the solar system has a disk formation, each planet, viewed from Earth, follows roughly the same path. Each planet has a different sidereal time, the time it takes to make one full revolution of the Sun. So each planet has different time periods in the sky. Mercury takes 88 days to rotate the Sun, Pluto takes more than 250 years.

As we have seen, it is these planetary positions that determine astrology, but we also know these planetary positions are only time periods. The stars and the planets are but a gigantic time map or clock in the sky. Man's ingenuity has enabled him to adapt the time periods of the planets to suit his mythology and his environment.

Back to Ancient Times

We have already established that cycles exist. We have seen that these cycles have been going on for hundreds and thousands of years.

Let us go back 6,000 years. Imagine you are an astronomer of that time. You have just experienced a particular abundance of pheasant. (You were not aware of it but that pheasant had a cycle of abundance of 5.91 years.) As you study the heavens you note Jupiter is in Taurus. Twelve years later Jupiter is in Taurus once more. (Jupiter has a sidereal period of 11.86 years.) Once again you have had an abundance of pheasant. Would you not put two and two together and make five? So Jupiter becomes the 'Greater Benefic' of the heavens. Whether or not modern man would make those assumptions I do not know, but I feel sure that our ancestors did.

Saturn, with its sidereal time of nearly thirty years, has been termed the bringer of old age, and it is not difficult to see how this was conceived. Uranus has a sidereal period of 84 years, thus it spends seven years in each sign. The astrologer has used this fact to establish the planetary ages of man. Thus man convinced himself that the planets caused events on Earth. He would have to come to this inevitable conclusion. The philosophy that the planets influence us has been handed down from generation to generation.

Man also assumed that the Earth was the centre of the solar system. It was not until relatively recently that we knew otherwise. The fact that astrology today still calculates the natal chart on the premise that the Earth is at the centre of the solar system speaks volumes about the rigid traditions that structure astrology. This rigidity allows no freedom to explore other possibilities than the dogma that the planets influence us — I maintain they do not.

The Astrologer's Dilemma

Man's adaptation of this time map in the heavens has brought with it a number of problems. It can be said that the very adaptation is the root of the problem. A typical example of this problem that the astrologer inherited is the two-dimensional picture the astrologer enforces upon himself when he assumes the Earth is the centre of the solar system. A good example of this is the 'retrograde' planet. Planets do not change their direction, yet sometimes it seems that they are in reverse and are going backwards. This is because when one views them from the Earth the angle at which we see them in relation to their orbit makes it appear, in the two-dimensional frame, as if they are going backwards. When this occurs the astrologer terms that planet as being 'retrograde'. In astrology the significance placed on a retrograde planet is, to say the least, confused. Some feel it has karmic significance. I feel it is hogwash. Certainly it clouds the issue, it confuses the picture.

For example, in the chapter 'A Small Discovery' it was the fact that Mercury had gone retrograde during the month of March 1933 that confused and clouded my picture of the true cause of the phenomena. The retrograde motion of Mercury caused considerable distortion to the results I initially obtained. Why the astrologer persists with such an archaic system when better methods could easily be developed is a mystery to me. It is this adaptation of a primitive two-dimensional view of the solar system that causes the astrologer so much trouble. It is this that forces him to choose whether to use the Equal House system, the Placidus House system or whatever.

The map of the heavens can be used as a time map. Astrology has proved that much. But there are limits as to how far one can adapt things. The Precession of the Equinoxes demonstrates that the system is out of date. The astrologer's dilemma of Sidereal versus Tropical is only to be expected.

For a long time now astrology has been trying to stretch the limits of this adaptation. Unfortunately they do not seem all that elastic.

The Harmonic Relationship

You will recall in the chapter on cycles, we discussed cycles that have a time period of 5.91 years, very close to the 2nd harmonic of the sidereal period of Jupiter. So if Jupiter was in Aries when the 5.91 year cycle turned, it would be in Libra when the cycle turned again, Jupiter's position in the Zodiac thus indicating the relevant phase of the cycle in the scheme of things. Why? Because one is a harmonic of the other. For example, within the 5.91 year cycles is a cycle of copper prices. If one had a characteristic shape of that cycle plotted on an XY graph, then the position of Jupiter in the Zodiac between Aries and Libra would represent the X axis of the graph. It is the harmonic relationship that is the key.

Look at the example of the 11 year cycle of accentuated characteristics, (in the chapter 'A Small Discovery') and the sidereal period of Mercury. Once again we have this harmonic relationship. It is the harmonic relationship of the time periods of the planets to the Cycles of Time that has enabled astrology to function over the centuries.

Again with Uranus and its sidereal period of 84 years, it has a direct harmonic relationship with that seven year cycle in our emotions.

Planetary Symbolism

Next in this debate on cycles versus planetary motion, there is the question of planetary symbolism. Can it be shown that there is both a symbolic and a harmonic relationship between the planets and the Cycles of Time? The answer is — Yes!

Take the case of Jupiter. Both a symbolic and a harmonic relationship can be demonstrated. Firstly, Jupiter has a sidereal period of 11.86 years. That is almost precisely twice 5.91. In other words, the 5.91 year cycle is the second harmonic of the sidereal period of Jupiter. A direct harmonic relationship. Secondly, if one scans the 5.91 year cycles it is evident that they are nearly always associated with abundance and prosperity. Stock prices, cotton prices, copper prices, grouse abundance, etc. One cycle of particular interest is the cycle of business failures (inverted). The inverted cycle of business failures means that when business failures were at their lowest point, all of the other cycles would be at their highest point. This cycle precisely demonstrates an association between the symbolic nature of Jupiter the planet of abundance and the 5.91 year cycles.

The Great Depression of 1990

Further in this matter of planetary symbolism, Dr Ravi Batra in his book *The Great Depression of 1990* demonstrates many cycles to justify his prediction that the world is approaching a great depression in 1990. It is not my aim to upstage Dr Batra, but there is one aspect that he did not include. Indeed any responsible economic analyst would not have included it, for it is 'Astrological'. However this book ties astrology to the same cycles that Dr Batra would use. We have seen that cycles are at the core of astrology, so now let us use that astrological symbolism with Dr Batra's cycles.

Dr Batra shows that there is a cycle of depressions that is of a 30-year duration, a 30 year period that the orbit of Saturn illustrates. He shows that there was a depression in 1780, 1840, 1870 and 1930. Depicted as a graph one can see that the years

1810, 1900 and 1960 missed having a depression. The purist might argue that 1990 may also miss a depression. However, Dr Batra covers that aspect with much other supporting evidence. One aspect he does not show, an aspect that depicts the gravity of the situation, is what astrology shows us about the forces that have joined forces to create this final crash. For some time now the cycle that the planet Neptune represents has been in a phase that affects the public sector of our lives. Neptune represents cloudiness and distortions to reality.

In February of 1988 it was joined by two other cycles. The cycle that the orbit of Uranus depicts, and the cycle that the orbit of Saturn illustrates. The orbit of Saturn gives us the timing of this depression and its symbolism denotes the repressions and limitations inherent in its development. The symbolism of the cycle that Uranus depicts is one of sudden shocks, of abruptness. Put all of these influences together and you have Neptune cycles setting a scene of illusions and deceptions, the Saturn cycles of limitations and repressions and finally the Uranian cycles bringing abrupt and sudden shocks. One further point — Uranus symbolises electronics and modern technology. It will be the world wide computer linkups, the global television satellite broadcasting and the use of computers for 'Program Trading' that will precipitate us into stock market disasters.

The satellite television broadcasts give us plenty of time to become apprehensive about financial markets in faraway parts of the world. For as distant markets open, the downward trend of stocks and shares precipitates a wave of gloom, a Spring tide of apprehension that perceptibly circum-navigates the globe. The employment of computers to automatically buy and sell on the markets leaves the individual investor little or no time to avoid those sudden market crashes. It is true that today's markets employ computer controlled 'Circuit Breakers' to avert recurrences of the 1929 disaster. However, if sufficient shocks are experienced there may be little that governments or institutions can do to avert this looming financial catastrophe.

It is fair comment to say that the scene is set for a major

recession, the inescapable truth is that there is a limit to how much profit can be realised on an investment, the piper must be paid eventually.

The last piece of evidence concerns the one discernible weak link in this argument. The fact that the years 1900 and 1960 did not result in depressions yet the cycle of depressions is apparently 30 years long — Why?

Analysis reveals that the orbit of Jupiter with its sidereal period of roughly 12 years divides neatly into the 30 year span of the cycle of economic depression. Jupiter epitomises cycles of abundance and prosperity, illustrating, by harmonics, the 5.91 year cycles. However, in addition, the timing of Jupiter's orbit appears to have a separate significance in its own right. During the 1930 depression the orbit of Jupiter was in Cancer. This positions the Jupiter cycle 180 degrees to the Saturn cycle of depressions, in other words, in direct opposition to Saturn. The Jupiter cycle of abundance thus at a low, combining with the Saturn cycle of depression and limitation to create — a depression! During both 1900 and 1960 the Jupiter cycle was at a high, in Capricorn, thus cancelling the effects of the Saturn cycle, the result — no depression.

This evidence clearly demonstrates the cyclic influences that are shaping our lives, it clearly exhibits the dramatic effect cycles can have. This is decisive confirmation of the connection between cycles and planetary motion. It illustrates a symbolism evolved from thousands of years of Man's observation.

The Many Indicators Combine

Recognise that it is the economic indicators and the movement of the planets showing us that we are rapidly approaching a worldwide economic recession. The inherited wisdom of countless astrologers permits us to get a better perspective on these cycles, these forces, that continually seem to reflect, or perhaps, even create, the intricate financial maze, this tangled web we have weaved for ourselves.

The vagaries and deceptions of Neptune, the abruptness of

Uranus, the limitations of Saturn, the Saturn cycle of depressions, the negative phase of Jupiter, the computer controlled international markets, stock markets trading by computer programme and the cyclic similarities to the 1922 crash — they do not leave much room for doubt about an imminent economic disaster.

Is It All Just Coincidence?

1. Is it coincidence that the economic indicators leading up to 1990 are virtually identical to those leading to 1930?

2. Is it coincidence that Saturn's orbital period matches exactly the cycle of depressions and that Saturn's symbolic nature is precisely that of repression and depression? Is it coincidence that Saturn is in the exact part of the Zodiac for this event to occur.

3. Is it coincidence that Jupiter's orbit and Jupiter's symbolic nature of expansion is precisely that to either augment or cancel the effects of a depression? Is it coincidence that Jupiter was in the exact position in the Zodiac in 1870, 1900, 1930 and 1960 to give those results?

4. Is it coincidence that unlike the 1929 crash, Uranian cycles now enter the scene. Uranus symbolising computer linkups, television and sudden, abrupt crashes? Those sudden inexplicable financial shocks that we have been experiencing for some time!

5. Is it coincidence that to sew the whole thing up the Neptune cycles also enter with their attendant symbolic nature of illusion, nebulousness, and deception. Neptune is exactly where one would expect it to be, to set a stage of cloudiness and vagary in these last confused chapters of our evolution.

6. Is it coincidence that the cycles that Saturn, Uranus, Neptune and Jupiter illustrate are all in their appointed positions NOW? Is it a coincidence that Pluto the planet of death and rebirth is in Scorpio, its home NOW? At this crucial time — the end of the

millennium — the end of the cycle of evolution.

Jupiter and the Sunspots

Lastly, we are left with the ultimate question. If cycles and planetary motion are related, which controls? The planets or the cycles? In other words, can it be that planetary motion causes these cycles or is planetary motion simply representative of these cycles by harmonic relationship?

The answer to that is quite clear. Let us refer to Jupiter and the 5.91 year cycles once more. Mr Dewey found correspondence between sunspots and the 5.91 year cycles. We must bear in mind at this point that the 5.91 year sunspot cycle is not the main cycle of sunspots. The main cycle, universally recognised, is eleven years in duration. Jupiter has no connection with this 11-year cycle. It simply exhibits synchronism with the 5.91 year cycles. It follows then that Jupiter cannot cause sunspots. To my mind there can be no question. The orbit of Jupiter does not cause sunspots, therefore planetary motion does not cause cycles.

Following from that, then, planetary motion does not affect our behaviour, our fate, our destiny or anything whatsoever. However, it can by harmonic relationship indicate these things. This is what astrology has done for centuries.

Enter Numerology

So far in this discussion we have not brought numerology into the picture. However, now you will see that numerology provides the cornerstone of the argument.

John Addey has shown the connection between astrology and numerology by the harmonic relationships of the astrological natal chart. He also demonstrated the harmonic synthesis of the work done by the Gauquelins.

In short, by applying scientific theory to determine the validity of astrology, the truth emerged that the rhythms of cycles can be seen as being in harmony one with the other. In other words, John Addey showed that the harmonics he demonstrated were a visible expression of the Pythagorean concept of numbers. He demonstrated the music of the heavenly spheres within the birthchart. Thus it is that numerology and the Pythagorean concept of numbers form the foundations upon which we may build this concept of the cycles of astrology.

It is as Pythagoras said: 'Evolution is the law of life, Number is the law of the Universe, Unity is the law of God.'

Consider the Evidence

Let us now stop and take stock of this argument concerning astrology and the Cycles of Time:

One: from the evidence presented on cycles, even the most skeptical would admit that this was conclusive, statistical proof of some entity that influenced or directed the course of events. These cycles are documentary statistical evidence of some force or influence in our daily lives. In short, cycles exist, they influence, they direct — there is no doubt.

Two: we have seen that there are cycles of emotions. We have seen a causal link between cycles and aspects of personality.

Three: the evidence on cycles shows them to be both repetitive and of regular rhythm. Our records demonstrate that cycles have been recorded for centuries. There is no reason to suppose that they have not continued for thousands and millions of years. On the contrary, the evidence of planetary motion and sunspots, which also must be seen as cycles, suggests that cycles have continued since creation. In view of the regularity of rhythms and their history, cycles must be predictable.

Four: astrology has evolved from the dim and distant past. It has been banned, banished, outlawed and persecuted. Still it persists and still it increases. It must operate from a central core of truth. Astrology is the study of planetary motion in the ecliptic, therefore astrology is the study of the time periods of the planets. Astrology can be called a study of the *cycles* of the planets, indeed astrologers tell us astrology is the study of cycles.

Five: we have seen that there is a harmonic relationship between the sidereal time of the planets and cycles.

We have seen that not only is there a harmonic relationship, there is also a symbolic relationship between planets and the cycles to which they have that harmonic relationship.

We have seen that there is a direct relationship between the orbit of Uranus and the seven-year cycle of man.

We have seen that there is a harmonic relationship between astrology and the symbolism of numbers (Numerology).

We have seen that there is a harmonic relationship between numerology and the sidereal period of the planets.

Six: we have seen a harmonic relationship between the sidereal time of Jupiter, the 5.91 year cycle of sunspots and cycles of prices and abundance on Earth.

We have seen a direct relationship between the orbit of Saturn and the cycle of economic depression.

We have seen that Jupiter's sidereal position does not cause sunspots.

Conclusion

There can be only one conclusion. The ancient study of astrology and the modern study of cycles are one and the same. Astrology works because man has made it work. The stars are but a giant time map in the sky. Man's ingenuity has enabled him to adapt the time periods of the planets to relate to the events that he has seen around him, those events being controlled or synchronised by the Cycles of Time.

In short, astrology and the Cycles of Time must be the same entity.

To Those Still Unconvinced

If you feel at this point that the case for astrology and cycles being the same entity has not been shown, then consider this last bit of common-sense.

We have seen that cycles are hard evidence and are predictable. We have seen that astrology works, but has no proof. We have seen that numerology works, but has no proof. Is it conceivable, is it likely, that these three entities operate side by side and are not the same? They are the same, they must be the same. We are simply seeing the same entity from three separate aspects. They are but three faces of the same diamond — The Cycles of Time.

Summing Up

From the evidence presented it is clear that astrology functions because of a harmonic relationship of the movement of the planets and these Cycles of Time. Similarly, numerology is but a harmonic synthesis of those same time periods.

The hard part, the difficulty, comes in the acceptance that these things are not some vagary. They are in reality definitive, for these things that are apparently supernatural are, in truth, predictions born out of fact.

The Moment of Time

The great psychiatrist Carl Jung said: 'Whatever is born or done in a moment of time, has the qualities of this moment of time.' I believe that it is around this one issue that the whole matter rests.

However, have we not just seen that astrology must work and is not Jung's statement implicit in any acceptance of astrology? Then it follows that Jung's statement must be true.

We can then, by the experience of astrology, state: whatever is of a moment of time has the qualities of that moment of time.

The Point in a Cycle

From this then can we not say: 'Whatever is born or done in a point in a cycle has the qualities of that point in the cycle.' In other words, the moment, point or phase of a cycle exhibits the qualities of the moment of time in that cycle.

The Collective of Cycles
Leaving us time to digest that aspect, let us now go back a moment to cycles.

During our study of cycles it was obvious that they are continuing at this moment; however, you will remember that there were many time periods of these cycles. It follows, therefore, that these cycles are all running concurrently or, if you like, side by side. Then from the above can we not say that: whatever is born or done at a moment of time has the collective qualities of all of the points of all of the cycles of that moment of time.

Cycle Analysis
To look at cycles in this manner implies that at any moment in time we may judge its quality to any other by viewing the phase relationships between differing cycles. It implies that we may assess any moment in time for any individual by analysing the phases of the cycles of the later time to the phases of the cycles of the birthdate.

The Microcosm and the Macrocosm
To put this another way, the character of a moment of time, the quality of a moment of time becomes the microcosm.

Recently I asked a group of experienced astrologers whether they considered an individual's anniversary of their birth day (i.e. their birthday), whether they considered the events of that day to represent the quality and character of that person's year ahead. In other words, the character of any birthday represents the microcosm and the year ahead represents the macrocosm. They could not answer; the principle remains however.

A New Potential
The dramatic aspect of what I am proposing is that

astrology is a historical demonstration of statistical analysis. You could say that our statistical trends indicate our astrological potential. As a result it should be possible to accurately predict the vagaries of the human factor from the variations in our statistical records. The possibilities of this approach are endless and the potential for development essentially infinite.

Analysis of the Collective

Further implications of this type of analysis indicate the eventual integration of the human factor into market statistics. A database could be assembled that combined statistics, astrological and numerological symbolism and the techniques of astrological aspect analysis. A further identification of cycles and planetary symbolism evolved, so this would also augment the growing database. Principles of analysis would probably be not unlike those employed with Biorhythm analysis but on a vastly larger scale.

Such a database could find instant application in marketing, politics, industry, labour relations, sociology, psychology, psychiatry, medicine, administration, local government, entertainment, law enforcement, etc. Groups such as the UK Cycles Network, an informal body of businessmen, are starting to emerge. In the USA, forecasting the fluctuations of bullion have met with considerable success.

The Astrology of Today

Nothing in this book will change anything. Today's astrologer will still continue to prepare his natal chart in the same way that he has always done. Nothing radical is about to take place. The purpose of this book is to show the viability of a concept. I believe that has been achieved. I believe this book identifies the potential we have in our statistical records. However, whilst our heads are in the clouds looking for planetary influence, we are not likely to notice that evidence that has grown around our feet.

Chapter 17

The Future

'Another Troy must rise and set,
Another lineage feed the crow,
Another Argo's painted prow
Drive to a flashier bauble yet
The Roman Empire stood appalled:
It dropped the reigns of peace and war
When that fierce virgin and her Star
Out of the fabulous darkness called.'

W.B. Yeats

The Jehovah's Witness

A few weeks ago, two ladies called at my front door. They were Jehovah's Witnesses seeking to redeem my soul. Talking to them for a while it became quite clear that they were very serious about their mission and not just a little afraid. It soon became obvious that they were disgusted and appalled at this world we live in. They found it wicked and perverted, corrupt and dishonest.

I tried to modify their terrible conviction that humanity was on the verge of destroying itself. I tried to show them that we were only coming to the end of a cycle and not the end of the world. Their gloom was insistent, their outlook morbidly set in concrete. No words of mine were going to dissuade them, to change this terrible fatalism. It appears that it is the belief of the Jehovah's Witness that out of nearly four billion people alive today, only 144,000 will survive the holocaust, the Jehovah's Witnesses being the chosen few.

The Jehovah's Witnesses are not the only religious sect to believe the Bible shows us the end of the world. The 'Born Again Christians' are also of the same opinion, believing that in the end they will be lifted up into the clouds while the rest of us perish on the earth.

The Nation of Israel

Hal Lindsay, in his book *The Late Great Planet Earth*, cites many prophecies from the Bible to show the end of things is near. One of these, he says, tells us the major sign of the end of the world was the setting up of the nation of Israel in 1948. To quote Hal Lindsay: 'The one event which many Bible students in the past overlooked was this paramount prophetic sign; Israel had to be a nation again in the land of its forefathers. Israel a nation — a dream for so many years, made a reality on 14 May 1948 when David Ben Gurion read the Declaration of Independence announcing the establishment of a Jewish nation to be known as the State of Israel. In 1949, Prime Minister Ben Gurion said that Israel's policy "consists of bringing all Jews to Israel . . . we are still at the beginning".'

Nostradamus

Nostradamus, the world famous seer of the seventeenth century, is renowned for his prophecies. Whereas some have had startling accuracy, the majority have been too vague to be proved wrong. It is the nature of man to try and make a prophecy fit the circumstance. Thus if a prophecy is vague or ambiguous, man will be sure that it is to his time that the words refer. As a result the name of Nostradamus has come down to us, reverberating from decade to decade and from century to century.

Pertinent to the issue is Quatrain II 71, a good example of this vagary:

> The exiles come to Sicily
> Deliverance from hunger and foreign control
> In the dawn the Celts fail them
> Life preserved by reason, the King joins.

Could it be that Nostradamus was alluding to the foundation of Israel despite British indifference?

The Importance of Israel

The importance of Israel in the scheme of things is more

than just Biblical prophecy. Nearly 2,000 years ago a cycle started. Two thousand years, a place called Masada, and a point beyond which an Israeli will never go.

Masada

Masada is a boat-shaped plateau in the eastern Judaean desert. Herod built a fortress for the Romans at Masada, a fortress that a century later the Romans would have to retake.

During the Jewish uprisings against the Romans the fortress was surprised and taken by a group of Zealots, wiping out the garrison. The Zealots held the place for a number of years whilst the Romans poured legion upon legion to crush and put down all other rebellion in Israel. Masada however stood firm, and the small garrison of Zealots was swelled by other insurgents driven out from other parts of the beleaguered country.

Finally the Roman attention was drawn to this last bastion of the Jewish uprising, and so with some 15,000 men they put the place to siege. There were less than a thousand Jews defending Masada. After a long and protracted siege the Romans succeeded in setting fire to the fortifications. This fire was the turning point in the battle. Influenced by a freak wind peculiar to the area, it had suddenly changed direction, causing the defenses to burn rather than to repel the attackers. The Romans were overjoyed and celebrated. The Jews on the other hand took the thing to be a sign that they had displeased God, so in an incredible moment of fervour they resolved they would never be taken. Drawing lots, ten men were selected as executioners. Every man in the garrison then went back to their families and whilst caressing and loving them, put their own wives and children to the sword. The ten executioners then put the remaining garrison to the sword, finally running themselves through. Thus when the Romans broke through and took the place in the morning, all they found was a woman and her two children hiding in a cave, and a dead, dead garrison.

Masada the Legend

So Masada became a legend. This incredible mass suicide became a statement. The Jews trapped in their mountain fortress, the slaughter of their women and children, was the ultimate sacrifice, it was Masada.

So to the present day, when Masada can still truly be called the rallying point of the Israeli nation. Does not every new member of the Israeli armed forces take his or her oath on that mountain fortress, on Masada? Do they not vow that they will never again be taken? And so it is, therefore, that somewhere in the Sinai desert lies a nuclear installation that ensures that the Israeli nation will never be taken. A construction truly in the spirit of Masada, a construction that could seal the fate of Mankind.

Thus the Biblical prophecy about the significance of Israel is much more than just being the seat of Middle-Eastern unrest.

The Second Coming of Christ

Returning to Hal Lindsay and *The Late Great Planet Earth*, he predicts a World War III and the major event — the second coming of Christ. He cites Micah 4:1-3

1. But in the last days it shall come to pass, that the mountain of the house of the LORD shall be established in the top of the mountains, and shall be exalted about the hills: and people shall flow unto it.
2. And many nations shall come, and say, Come, and let us go up to the mountain of the LORD, and to the house of the God of Jacob; and he will teach us of his ways, and we will walk in his paths: for the law shall go forth of Zion, and the word of the LORD from Jerusalem.
3. And he shall judge among many people, and rebuke strong nations afar off; and they shall beat their swords into plowshares, and their spears into pruning hooks: nation shall not lift up a sword against nation, neither shall they learn war any more.

The Cycle of Entropy

Hal Lindsay ends the book: 'As we see the world becoming more chaotic, we can be "steadfast" and "immovable", because we know where it is going and where we are going. We know that Christ will protect us until His purpose is finished and then He will take us to be with Himself. We can "abound in His work" as we trust him to work in us and know that it is not in vain because He will give us rewards to enjoy forever for every work of faith. So let us seek to reach our family, our friends, and our acquaintances with the Gospel with all the strength He gives us. The time is short.

'In the early centuries, the Christians had a word for greeting and departing; it was the word "marantha", which means "the Lord is coming soon". We can think of no better way with which to say good-by — MARANTHA.'

It is evident that a good proportion of the thinking population believes that things are getting worse, to quote Hal Lindsay — 'more chaotic'. Although not directly saying it, they infer that we live under a law of entropy — a law that states everything gets worse. I believe that it is not a law of entropy but a cycle of entropy, an entropy that is in reality a cycle of evolution. The dictionary definition of entropy is: 'A measure of the state of disorder in a system'.

It is obvious that there is a parallel between today's society and this law of thermodynamics. For as life becomes more complex and the pace increases, do we not find it increasingly difficult to establish a spiritual base to our lives. Do we not find that our standards are constantly being eroded? Do we not find that the only constant is change itself, and is not that change happening at an ever increasing rate? Have we not seen our moral standards diminishing day by day? Have we not seen crimes of violence and unspeakable brutality on the increase? Have we not seen disorder, disruption and moral decay everywhere?

Why? Because we are at the end of the cycle of entropy, we are about to enter a new cycle of evolution.

The Last Days

The emphasis placed on the words 'In the last days' or 'The end of the world' puts us in a negative phase before we start. It puts us down before we have a chance to get up. Hal Lindsay says: 'As the battle of Armageddon reaches its awful climax and it appears that all life will be destroyed on earth — in this very moment Jesus Christ will return and save man from self extinction.'

Are we the First Civilisation?

It is all very well to hope that the almighty will save us. It is all very well to have faith and to trust in the Lord. But how many other civilisations have followed that route? Charles Berlitz in his book *The Bermuda Triangle* cites: 'In the course of exploratory digging in southern Iraq in 1947, layers of culture were successively cored into by what one might call an archaeological mine shaft. Starting from the present ground level, the excavation passed the ancient city culture levels of Babylonia, Chaldea and Sumer, with flood levels between different ages of city culture, then the first village levels, then a level corresponding to that of primitive farmers at the time of 6,000 to 7,000 BC, and below that indications of a herdsman culture, and finally a time era was reached corresponding to the Magdelanian or cave culture of about 16,000 years ago. Still farther down, at the bottom of all levels, a floor of fused glass was revealed, similar to nowhere else but the desert floor in New Mexico after the blasts which inaugurated our present atomic era.'

The Cycle of Evolution

If we are to believe the implications of the last quotation, it would seem that more than 16,000 years ago in the area we now call Iraq there was a civilisation that had achieved a technology equal to ours, at least in the field of nuclear physics. Who were they? Did they exist? We do not know.

Plato stated that there have been many destructions of

mankind. The ancient religions of India tell us there are nine crises of mankind. A cyclic theory of civilisation has been passed down to us from the ancient world. Many talk today about the Atlantean civilisation or the Lemurian civilisation.

The dinosaurs vanished from the earth 65 million years ago. That is a very long time for us to be the first civilisation since then.

The facts are that a cyclic theory of evolution is not only possible but probable. It would seem that we are at the end of such a cycle at this very moment in time.

We Must Help Ourselves

The important thing to bear in mind is that we are aware of it, it has been brought to our attention. Thus by being aware of it, it is up to us to do something about it. We cannot simply hope on a prophecy that Christ will arrive for a second time and save us from exterminating ourselves. We have the knowledge, we have the means, we must ourselves ensure that we survive. To quote Jean De La Fontaine (1621-1695) 'Aide-toi, le ciel t'aidera' (Help yourself, and heaven will help you).

The Turning Point

During the chapter on cycles we noted the very close similarity of conditions in the years leading up to a depression. These periods have so much in common that they are compelling in their demonstration of cyclic events. If the conditions leading to an event have similarity, then it is logic that the conditions succeeding that event should also exhibit similarities.

Just under ten years (9.9 years) from the 1929 crash, World War II started. If a depression occurs in late 89 then 9.9 years later puts us at around July 1999. One of the very few examples where Nostradamus was very specific about dates was Quatrain 1072 where he indicates July 1999 as having fateful significance:

> The year 1999, seventh month,
> From the sky will come a great King of Terror:

To bring back to life the great King of the Mongols,
Before and after Mars to reign by good luck.

The term 'great King of the Mongols' would refer to Genghis
Khan. In Quatrain 672 Nostradamus again refers to the time at
the turn of the millennium:

Mars and the sceptre will be found conjoined
Under Cancer calamitous war:
Shortly afterwards a new king will be annointed,
One who for a long time will pacify the earth.

Lines 1 and 2 translated mean when Mars and Jupiter are
conjunct in Cancer. Wollner (1926, p.59) indicates that such a
conjunction will only take place on 21 June, 2002.

The timing of these events precisely at the turn of the
millennium has so much significance, significance in the
symbology of the numerology of cycles. It is an indicator of the
change in the structure and the manifestation of mankind
itself.

The Awakening
It is a tragic fact that when a civilisation becomes fully
developed, individuals and institutions forget their origins,
materialism becomes triumphant and the ego no longer walks
hand in hand with the soul. It seems that humanity can only be
awakened by an apocalypse, by a shattering of the tinted
windows to reality, by ripping away the veils of apathy.

All nations, indeed civilisations, are founded on visions. We
have lost sight of ours. Those visions represent our spirituality,
our ideals, our souls. They can suffer only so much at the
pragmatic hand of materialism. Eventually they must rise up in
revolt, to scream out 'an end to this madness, this insanity'.

The New Millennium
The cycles have shown us that numerology is valid and
it works. Now let numerology work for us in understanding the
changing face of humanity at a time following what has to be a

war to end wars, for centuries at least.

Firstly, the very fact that all this is happening at the turn of the millennium signifies the transition from the millennium of the 1 to the millennium of the 2 in the mind of man.

The Millennium of Woman

This millennium has been the millennium of the number 1, the male, the masculine, the phallic. The next millennium is the millennium of the number 2, the female, the feminine.

Whereas this millennium has seen wars upon wars, the next will not be that way. This millennium is the millennium of the male, the millennium of the phallus, a millennium of rise and fall. The next will still have cycles but they will be cycles of the female, cycles of eternal recurrence, the vulva bleeds and it heals. Have we not seen in this last century of the millennium the rise of the female, of the Suffragettes, of equal rights for women? Have we not seen a rise in the divorce rate as woman seeks equal rights with man and change becomes a necessity? Not change of the partner, but change in the perception of the union, the true concept of equality. This century has been associated with the demise of marriage. How much better it is to think of it as the dawn of the democracy of marriage.

So on to the second millennium, possibly through the rigours of a terrible war, but not to extermination. Instead to an awareness of love, to a time of peace. The time of woman, the millennium of the female and the feminine.

The Millennium of the 2

What will the people of the twenty-first century be like? Numerology shows us that the make-up of the population will change markedly. Today everyone has a 1 in their birthdate, in the next millennium only 60-70% will be so equipped. The absence of the 1 will place more emphasis in other areas and reduce the number of 'I Am's' in the community. Thus the community is likely to be more integrated, less individualistic.

This does not mean that the individualists will not be around; they will, but in lesser numbers. The predominance of the 2 in the chart will make everyone more intuitive, more aware of each other, more co-operative. Another immediate change will be the number 9 missing from a majority of charts, this indicating an inherent fear of expressing the emotions. For example, compare the nineteenth century people with those of today. To understand fully the implications and significance of this change, let us briefly look at the positives and negatives of the number 2.

Positives: love, service, gentleness, harmony, adaptability, diplomacy, charm, friendliness, rhythm, music, receptivity, co-operation, consideration of others.

Negatives: deception, cruelty, cowardice, bad temper, slyness, pessimism, shyness, discontent, slackness, apathy, vacillation, lies.

The Angelic Offspring

Once again the vagary of Nostradamus enters the scene with Quatrain X.42:

> The human realm of angelic offspring,
> Causes lasting peace and unity
> War subdues under its control
> Peace is maintained for a long time

The key to this quatrain is the word 'angelic'. The confusing translation becomes crystal clear when one sees it in the light of the dramatic change of character introduced when we enter the twenty-first century.

The Tribes of New Guinea

The tribes of New Guinea give us patterns as to the characters of different societies. To quote Dr H.J. Eysenck: 'Among the Arapesh, a mountain-dwelling people in New Guinea, we find that both men and women show what we would call feminine traits. This group appears to have outlawed competition, aggressiveness and dominant behaviour and to have replaced these with mutual trust and affection. There is very little stress on age or sex differences in their society, which comes as near, perhaps, as any to the ideals of a classless society. Even the children's games are non-competitive and any fights which arise are immediately broken up by adults. Observers frequently refer to the Arapesh as "One big happy family". At the opposite extreme, take the Mundugumor, a cannibal tribe in New Guinea. There, both men and women show what are considered masculine traits. They are ruthless, violent, domineering, aggressive and ready to fight at the slightest provocation. Right from the beginning the child is born into a hostile world, weaned early, treated to blows and often killed by the mother, who shows no sign of that hypothetical maternal instinct which we consider so natural and normal a feature of femininity. An actual reverse of sex attitudes is found amongst the Tchambuli. Here the woman is the dominant, impersonal, managing partner and the man the less responsible and emotionally dependent partner. It is the woman that makes the sexual choice; it is the man who is chosen. Women get along well with each other; men are 'catty' about other men, suspicious and distrustful. Because of their dependence on women for security the men are shy, sensitive and subservient; they engage in artistic and other "feminine" activities, such as dancing, weaving and painting.'

Let us hope that the prophetic words of Nostradamus, and the word 'angelic', indicate that we are moving to be that of the Arapesh. To quote the Bible once more, Matthew 5,5: 'Blessed are the meek: for they shall inherit the earth.'

The Cycle of Population

Sir Fred Hoyle is one of the world's foremost cosmologists. In his book *Ten Faces of the Universe* he postulates that there is a cycle of human productivity and population, a cycle dependent on the ability of the race to procreate. This cycle would have shape much akin to that of surf on the beach, to cite his words, 'Then nothing will prevent our current wave of productivity and population from breaking . . .' And he continues: '. . . Probably around the year 2025, as I mentioned earlier. A succeeding Dark Age will follow, possibly lasting for several centuries.'

Fred Hoyle postulates that around 2025, with the current patterns of growth, the cycle of population would break. He has more to say: 'Like the Dark Age following the collapse of the Roman Empire, this new Dark Age will probably be an age of invention, an age with more individual freedom than we experience today, an age that is quiet and pleasant to live in.'

An age quiet, and pleasant to live in. Is it not reminiscent of the female of the species? The Millennium of the 2? The Arapesh? The meek inheriting the Earth?

Thus the numerology echoes the Bible, Fred Hoyle and Nostradamus and humanity recovers from the holocaust. However, nothing is predestined, nothing is written except the pattern of things. It is up to us what we do with this knowledge. Edgar Cayce, America's 'Sleeping Clairvoyant', now dead for forty years, told tales of the Atlantean civilisation. No one has hard evidence of the existence of such people yet we feel that they did exist. It is up to us to ensure that we leave more behind than a dream. Remember, the cycles will continue whether Man is here or not! Jupiter and Saturn will still orbit the Sun when Man is gone. It is what we do with our lives that counts — never forget:

> Aide-toi, le ciel t'aidera
> (Help yourself, and heaven will help you)

> Like as the damask rose you see,
> Or like the blossom on the tree,
> Or like the dainty flower of May,
> Or like the morning to the day,
> Or like the Sun, or like the shade,
> Or like the gourd which Jonas had —
> Even such is man, whose thread is spun,

Drawn out, and cut, and so is done,
The rose withers, the blossom blasteth,
The flower fades, the morning hasteth,
The Sun sets, the shade flies,
The gourd consumes; and man he dies.

From *Like as the Damask Rose You See* (Anon)

Chapter 18

The Church of Cycles

Where is that gateway to space and time?
Where everyone and thing together rhyme
That place that space that is not of time
Where everyone and thing must be sublime.

Search no longer did I hear you say?
Just stand and it will come your way?
For in the dawning of the breaking day
There is the glory of the infinite way.

Facing the Facts

By now, after reading this book, it must be evident that we are dealing with forces that are not only beyond our control but also almost beyond our comprehension. Throughout the ages astrology and numerology have been regarded as superstition, primarily because of an inability to conceive how they could work. This book demonstrates that both numerology and astrology represent cycles hidden within our statistics. That in essence makes both numerology and astrology representative of fact. They illustrate the trends in our statistics, moreover they illustrate these trends with a symbolism that has taken thousands of years to evolve. The purpose of this book is not so much to vindicate these two ancient sciences but fundamentally to draw attention to the existence of cycles themselves. Evidence of cycles exists within our statistics and historical records. They cannot, they must not be ignored any longer. If it can be shown, as in the last chapter, that the worst depression in our history is not only imminent but also unavoidable, is it not time that we formally acknowledge the existence of these trends and by so doing are able to take preventative measures to avoid such disasters in the future?

It is because not enough weight is placed on the evidence of these cycles that things are allowed to get out of hand. It is time we faced the facts, it is time we acknowledged that there are influences beyond our control. It is my belief that if we were not able to take remedial measures we would not have been given the knowledge in the first place. It is time homo sapiens got off the yellow brick road and took full account of the direction he is taking.

Until we study these cycles deeply and completely, until we bring them out into the open and accept them, until we fully acknowledge their influence, we are at their mercy. We are condemned by our own stupidity, by our own ignorance.

With a nuclear arsenal strategically placed around the globe how can we afford to ignore influences that might trigger a holocaust. It is up to all of us to do whatever we can to understand these forces. For our very survival if it be that we cannot seize the director's baton to the orchestra of our affairs, then we must, at least, know the tune that is playing.

The Scheme of Things

Our material world, our bodies, our cars, our televisions, our computers, our flora and fauna, the animal kingdom, they all exhibit cycles. Cycles are the scheme of things, from the ultrafast frequencies of cosmic radiation, to the billions of years for the cycles of the suns, they all are cycles.

Just as Saturn with its rings demonstrates the solar system, then so does the orbit of Saturn demonstrate the cycle of economic depressions on Earth. In other words, just as Saturn represents the Solar system in a geometric framework, then so does the orbit of Saturn represent events on earth in a time framework. Similarly for Jupiter, Mercury, Venus, Uranus, Mars, Neptune and Pluto. That is what astrology is — nothing else!

However, what it demonstrates is that we, as human beings, are intrinsically part of a much larger scheme of things than we thought. What it shows is that the directions we take in life are influenced in ways that we were not aware of. We have to become aware of these influences, we must understand them. For that is the scheme of things.

The Source

To our concepts that have to understand things in a three-dimensional solid framework, the origin of these cycles would have to remain an enigma, a mystery. For how can one hope to comprehend the enormity of a concept that ties together sunspots, the orbit of Jupiter and the price of pig iron on Earth. The concept is unbelievable but it is true, it is fact. It is this that makes it all the more unbelievable.

The enormity of this concept leaves one in awe, leaves one in a stupid daze. For how does one take in such things, how can the human mind envelop the vastness of such a scheme and where do we, as humans, fit in such a wonder? Where does one start to look for that origin, that source, out there in the vastness and infinity of space? Does one bow his head, get on his knees and pray? If so, to what? and where? and to what purpose?

There is a symbolism here that we must not miss, there are things we must realise that are beyond our understanding. The vastness, the enormity, the range and the origin of these cycles is a mystery we are not about to unravel.

The fact that these cycles operate on and affect us shows us that we are at the centre of things. For just as we look outwards to an infinity of space, so we can look inwards to the tiniest particle of matter. It is as though we are at the centre, we ourselves are the source. It is as though we are the microcosm, and the universe the macrocosm. Above the temple at Delphi are these words: Know Thyself.

It is as Pythagoras said: 'Man know thyself and thou shalt know the universe and God.'

The Cycle of Entropy

Two thousand years ago in Bethlehem a child was born. That birth marked the start of a new cycle for mankind, a cycle of Christianity, of humanity. The birth of Jesus Christ was so significant, so important that Man created a new dating system to mark forever that time in his memory. For Christ's coming was precisely in synchronism with the patterns of the Universe.

Does not his birth determine the very numbers, the precise numerals of Numerology? So the last pieces of the jigsaw fall in place and the words of Pythagoras echo again: 'Evolution is the law of life, Number is the law of the Universe, Unity is the law of God.'

Christ's message was abundantly clear. He came to tell us of love, to tell us to love our brothers, to turn the other cheek. To tell us of the unity and universal love of God's kingdom. Was not Jesus Christ then truly the son of God? Did not his coming begin a new cycle in the evolution of Man?

However, it is clear that nearly 2,000 years later this time is ending. For as this cycle accelerates to its rapid and dramatic conclusion, we heed less and less this vital message of Christ. We question and doubt the validity of orthodox religions. We no longer populate the churches. We ignore the crucial significance of his divine word. For we are in the rapids of the river of time, the swirling currents and eddies of change thrust and drag us from side to side, to and fro. We have put aside that crucial survival lesson of Christ — brotherly love. We ignore the edict of the unity of God and in so doing threaten our civilisation, our very race with extinction.

Alvin Toffler in his book *Future Shock* discusses what happens to people when they are subjected to change, how they adapt or fail to adapt. He describes change as an 'elemental force': 'the roaring current of change, a current so powerful today that it overturns institutions, shifts our values and shrivels our roots.'

Our technological development has been so rapid, so accelerated that our philosophy, our morality and our spirituality has not been able to keep pace with it. Take for instance the issues surrounding In Vitro fertilisation. There is no doubt that for a couple who are childless and can only expect to be so, In Vitro fertilisation is an almost ideal solution. However, with a very large proportion of the world's population having to practise strict birth control, is that not a moral dilemma? When the issue is extended to surrogate motherhood and cloning, are we not delving into matters that we are not equipped to handle? Are we not playing with fire?

It seems we have advanced along the technical road to the expense of all the other avenues open to us. We simply cannot make decisions about our future because we simply do not understand all the implications. Rapid development and change have led us to a position where our judgement is sorely impaired by our abysmal ignorance.

Although written nearly two decades ago, *Future Shock* highlights the predicament we now find ourselves in. Today things are so complex and interactive that a decision in one area of life overflows rapidly into all others. In the arena of big business the big get bigger and the small get smaller. This has advanced to the point where multinational corporations now hold sway, with the result that a business decision in London, New York or Tokyo dramatically affects the way of life in Auckland, Sydney or Hamburg, leaving the individuals affected with little or no say in the matter.

Profit is the governing factor in any business. Multinational corporations have grown to the size and proportions of small nations. Should profit be allowed to influence our sociological and ecological development? It is obvious that it should not, but it is equally obvious that it does!

Clemenceau said war is too serious a business to be left to the generals. For that matter, then, so is science to the scientists, government to the politicians and industry to big business.

The uncomfortable reality of technological change is that it has outstripped our sociological, our moral, our psychological abilities. We have too much power at our fingertips. We are running berserk, we are running wild. It was permissible for our ancestors to run wild, but we are running wild with a time bomb, a time bomb that has its detonator set quite precisely!

We blithely ignore these vast elemental forces, these cyclic currents that will drag us on to our own blind self destruction. We worship our material achievements in a fervour of competition, of thoughtless ego boosting. These cycles are within us, it will be we who bring about our own change, our own destruction. It will not be an alien invasion that determines Man's demise, he will manage that all by himself!

In the whole of World War II a total of two megatons of high explosive was dropped. Today one single bomb has that power. One single bomb has the power of all the high explosive dropped in the last war! There are enough devices stockpiled for a planned strategic attack on 15,000 targets around the world, a precisely calculated offensive that could be accomplished within the space of a single afternoon. It is calculated that more than two billion people would perish at that one time. Add to that the effect of a nuclear winter, and where does that leave mankind?

Scientists searching for other life in the cosmos, vainly look for signs of intelligence coming from the stars. It is recognised that there is a technological barrier through which a civilisation must pass to survive. The scientists seek this communication to prove that this barrier can be crossed, that others have passed through these gates of fire. The cycles show us quite clearly we are at those gates *now*. We must get through or perish. The evidence is in our grasp, the stark truth cannot be ignored. If we are to survive we must heed the message of these cycles.

Homo sapiens stands apart from all other animals for we have a cerebral cortex. We have the capability of conscious thought, the wonder of imagination, the power of design. We understand harmony, we comprehend the abstract, we rejoice in our humanity, the conscious awareness of the soul. Of all Man's towering achievements, none surpasses those of music. Consider for a moment the deep humanity and religious grandeur of Bach's St Matthew Passion, or Beethoven, the poet of heroism. Music has been written as beautiful as his but none that seems to transcend the boundaries of human limitations as does his. For it is in music that the intangible becomes reality, that the abstract transforms to harmony. It is in those mundane crotchets and quavers that the voice of the soul is heard, that our humanity is revealed.

From Bartok to Sibelius, Shakespeare to Shaw, Michelangelo to Rembrandt, Caruso to Callas, Pavlova to Nureyev, Newton to Einstein, Curie to Pasteur, do we not owe them something? Do we not owe them more than a glassy surface on some forgotten desert? We must recognise our inner spark, our inner flame. We must see the goodness in Man not the terror, the love not the hate. If we truly wish to survive we must show the inner spirit of Man, that which sets us apart from the beast!

Noah knew it, Abraham knew it, Solomon knew it, Buddha knew it, Christ knew it, Gandhi knew it and countless others have known it throughout time.

Unity is the law of God

Modern man must now learn it or perish — Universal love is the only way.

The Temple is Within Us

The Church of Cycles is within all of us. Have we not seen that we are all affected and influenced by these cycles? Are we not each one of us our own receiving station for these cycles? In the final analysis, what can these cycles be but a visible expression of the God force in action, a visible sign of the divine presence? Are they not the sign that all is not insanity? Are they not the sign that there is order, there is reason, there is purpose to this life?

Is it not evident from all this that there is a law of the universe, a law and an energy that is continuing and that we are part of? Are we not blessed to be given this knowledge, this awareness of purpose?

The Church of Cycles is within all of us, each one of us carries in him his own temple, his own place of awareness, his own purity and his own salvation.

I end this book with a poem that I hope sums it up.

May God go with you.

The Way

There comes a time when all must pray
When guidance of the spirit is the need
We search and search to find the way
Each path to find where it does lead

We hope that the palmist may show the way
We see if in numbers the answers are told
We hear what the astrologer has to say
We test the tarot for what it does hold

Some try the Runes to trust in those stones
Some feel the Cartouche may give an insight
And others may put their faith in the bones
Yet others may say that the cards can be right

Some will to their churches now turn
Some to the East may try for solutions
But most are bemused, in trying to learn
Many are bewildered, lost in confusions

The answers you see are not given in whole
The path you must take has no signposts to show
This life that we lead is but a test of the soul
Our choice is the way, we must falter or grow

For there can be no directions, no signpost to tell
There can be no predictions, or forecast for sure
This life after all is a test, or its hell
Our choice is the answer, to kill or to cure

To all those in doubt, lost or in sin
To all those bewildered, and out in the cold
Look not outside you, instead look within
You'll find that the answers you already do hold

For the soul in its journey through life after life
Knows the meaning and purpose of all our endeavour
Knows the reasons for living, the cause of our strife
Knows that love is the answer, for now and forever

For love is the power that is greatest of all
Love is the source, the pure, the divine
Love is the strength on which all can call
Love is God, the end of the line.

APPENDICES

Appendix I: A Brief Chronology

5000BC	Hunters engrave reindeer horns with phases of moon
2872BC	Sargon of Agade uses astrologers for prediction
2600BC	First Pyramid built by King Snefru, 4th Dynasty
1700 BC	Hammurabi extends Babylonian Empire
1650BC	Start of Mycenaean empire in Greece
1300BC	Rameses II fixes cardinal points of astrology
753BC	Foundation of Rome
700BC	Great Library at Nineveh founded
668BC	Earliest surviving horoscope
590BC	Pythagoras born at Sidon
429BC	Plato, Greek philosopher born
356BC	Alexander the Great builds empire from Athens to India
280BC	Berosus founds School of Astrology
63BC	Augustus has coins stamped with sign Capricorn
1AD	Birth of Christ
120AD	Claudius Ptomely, author of astrological textbook
330AD	Foundation of Constantinople by Roman Emperor Constantine
354AD	St Augustine starts purge of astrologers
400AD	Visigoths over-run Eastern Roman Empire
400AD	The Great Library at Alexandria destroyed
476AD	Last Roman Emperor deposed by the Huns
570AD	Mohammed, prophet and founder of Islam
743AD	Charlemagne, first Holy Roman Emperor
747AD	Capital of Islam moved from Damascus to Baghdad
800AD	Ibrahim Al Fazari invents Astrolabe
1000AD	Viking guard formed in Constantinople
1066AD	Normans conquer England
1099AD	First crusade captures Jerusalem
1125AD	University of Bologna founds Chair of Astrology
1125AD	St Thomas of Aquinas accepts concept of astrology
1162AD	Genghis Khan, founder of largest empire known
1225AD	Cambridge University founded
1250AD	Astrology taught at Cambridge University
1259AD	Chinese use gunpowder
1260AD	John of Hollywood writes textbook on astrology
1265AD	Dante uses astrological imagery

1280AD	Campanus invents a new method of house division
1291AD	Fall of Acre to Egyptian Sultan, Crusaders conquered
1340AD	Chaucer, English poet, uses astrology extensively
1414AD	Pope Sixtus IV first Astrologer Pope
1438AD	First Hapsburg Holy Roman Emperor
1453AD	Ottaman Turks capture Constantinople, ends Byzantine empire
1455AD	Gutanberg publishes Bible
1461AD	The Hundred Years War between France and England ends
1473AD	Copernicus dedicates work to Astrologer Pope Paul III
1483AD	Martin Luther born
1492AD	Columbus discovers the New World (America)
1492AD to 1503AD	Pope Alexander VI elected and together with his daughter Lucretia Borgia makes the papacy a great power
1492AD	The Spanish conquer Granada and expel Moors
1503AD	Nostradamus born Saint Reay, Provence, France
1511AD	Pope forms Holy League against France
1512AD	French defeat Holy League at Brescia and Ravenna
1514AD	Selim the Gris of Turkey, forty-year war with Persia
1519AD	Sir Thomas Moore publishes Utopia
1527AD	John Dee, Astrologer to Queen Elizabeth I
1538AD	Geradius Mercator publishes map of the world
1546AD	Tycho Brahe, Astronomer, Astrologer
1564AD	Galileo Galilei uses telescope
1564AD	Sir William Shakespeare extensively uses astrology
1566AD	Death of Nostradamus
1568AD	Tommaso Campanella, Astrologer
1571AD	Johannes Kepler, Astronomer, Astrologer
1577AD	Sir Francis Drake sails round the world
1602AD	William Lily, Astrologer born
1603AD	Placidus de Titis, inventor of Placidus system born
1620AD	Pilgrim Fathers sail from Plymouth
1642AD	Isaac Newton born
1738AD	Sir William Herschell born
1781AD	Uranus discoversd
1788AD	Settlement of Australia
1789AD	Start of French Revolution
1795AD	Richard Morrison, Astrologer born

1799AD	Napoleon seizes control of France
1814AD	Napoleon exiled to Elba
1831AD	Helena Blavatsky born — Theosophical Society
1846AD	Neptune discovered
1875AD	Carl Gustav Jung born
1875AD	Aleister Crowley born
1890AD	The Hermetic Order of the Golden Dawn
1914AD	World War I starts
1918AD	World War I ends
1920AD	John Addey, Astrologer born
1930AD	Pluto discovered
1939AD	World War II starts
1945AD	World War II ends
1950AD	Michel Gauquelin begins research into astrology
1957AD	Russian Sputnik I makes first space journey
1963AD	President Kennedy assassinated
1969AD	The first man lands on the moon
1975AD	Russians and Americans rendezvous in space
1977AD	The rings of Uranus discovered
1978AD	The moon of Pluto discovered
1979AD	Russians spend 175 days in space

Appendix II: The Celebrity List

A list of well known identities used in this book.

Celebrity	Birthday	Interest
Bud Abbott	Oct 2, 1898	Movies & TV
Quincy Adams	Jul 11, 1767	Historical
Brian Aherne	May 2, 1902	Movies & TV
Anna Maria Alberghetti	May 15, 1936	Movies & TV
Eddie Albert	Apr 22, 1908	Movies & TV
Muhammad Ali	Jan 18, 1942	Boxing
Fred Allen	May 31, 1894	Movies & TV
Rex Allen	Dec 31, 1922	Movies & TV
Steve Allen	Dec 26, 1921	Movies & TV
Woody Allen	Dec 1, 1935	Movies & TV
June Allyson	Oct 7, 1923	Movies & TV
Hardie Amies	Jul 17, 1909	Fashion
Hans Christian Anderson	Apr 21, 1805	Literature
Ursula Andress	Mar 19, 1936	Movies & TV
Dana Andrews	Jan 1, 1909	Movies & TV
Julie Andrews	Oct 1, 1935	Movies & TV
Ann-Margret	Apr 28, 1941	Movies & TV
Marie Antoinette	Nov 2, 1775	Historical
Eve Arden	Apr 30, 1912	Movies & TV
Harold Arlen	Feb 15, 1905	Popular music
Louis Armstrong	Jul 4, 1900	Popular music
Neil Armstrong	Aug 5, 1930	Astronaut
James Arness	May 26, 1923	Movies & TV
Desi Arnez	Mar 2, 1917	Movies & TV
Isaac Asimov	Jan 2, 1920	Literature
John Astin	Mar 30, 1930	Movies & TV
Mary Astor	May 3, 1906	Movies & TV
Richard Attenborough	Aug 29, 1923	Movies & TV
Jane Austen	Dec 16, 1775	Literature
Gene Autry	Sept 29, 1907	Movies & TV
Lew Ayres	Dec 28, 1908	Movies & TV
Lauren Bacall	Sep 16, 1924	Movies & TV

Frances Bacon	Jan 22, 1561	Historical
Joan Baez	Jan 9, 1941	Popular music
Carroll Baker	May 28, 1931	Movies & TV
John Bainbridge	Mar 12, 1913	Literature
John Logie Baird	Aug 13, 1888	Science
Lucille Ball	Aug 6, 1911	Movies & TV
Anne Bancroft	Sep 17, 1931	Movies & TV
Tallulah Bankhead	Jan 31, 1903	Movies & TV
Brigitte Bardot	Sep 28, 1934	Movies & TV
Gene Barry	Jun 14, 1921	Movies & TV
Lionel Barrymore	Apr 28, 1878	Movies & TV
Richard Basehart	Aug 31, 1914	Movies & TV
Shirley Bassey	Jan 8, 1937	Popular music
Anne Baxter	May 7, 1923	Movies & TV
Warner Baxter	Mar 29, 1891	Movies & TV
Warren Beatty	Mar 30, 1937	Movies & TV
Ludwig van Beethoven	Dec 16, 1770	Classical music
Menachem Begin	Aug 13, 1913	Government
Alexander Graham Bell	Mar 3, 1847	Science
Jean-Paul Belmondo	Apr 9, 1933	Movies & TV
William Bendix	Jan 14, 1906	Movies & TV
Joan Bennett	Feb 27, 1910	Movies & TV
Brook Benton	Sep 19, 1933	Popular music
Candice Bergen	May 9, 1946	Movies & TV
Polly Bergen	Jul 14, 1930	Movies & TV
Ingrid Bergman	Aug 29, 1915	Movies & TV
Milton Berle	Jul 12, 1908	Movies & TV
Irving Berlin	May 11, 1888	Popular music
Hector Berlioz	Dec 11, 1803	Classical music
Shelley Berman	Feb 3, 1924	Movies & TV
Sarah Bernhardt	Oct 22, 1844	Actress
Elmer Bernstein	Apr 4, 1922	Classical music
Leonard Bernstein	Aug 25, 1918	Classical music
Stephen Birmingham	May 28, 1931	Literature
Jacqueline Bisset	Sep 13, 1944	Movies & TV
Bill Bixby	Jan 22, 1934	Movies & TV
Georges Bizet	Oct 25, 1838	Classical music
Cilla Black	May 27, 1943	Popular music
Janet Blair	Apr 23, 1921	Movies & TV

Linda Blair	Jan 22, 1959	Movies & TV
Claire Bloom	Feb 15, 1931	Movies & TV
Ann Blyth	Aug 16, 1928	Movies & TV
Dirk Bogarde	Mar 29, 1921	Movies & TV
Humphrey Bogart	Jan 23, 1899	Movies & TV
Ray Bolger	Jan 10, 1904	Dancing
Ward Bond	Apr 9, 1903	Movies & TV
Pierre Bonnard	Oct 3, 1867	Painting & Art
Pat Boone	Jun 1, 1934	Popular music
Shirley Booth	Aug 30, 1907	Movies & TV
Ernest Borgnine	Jan 24, 1915	Movies & TV
Charles Boyer	Aug 28, 1899	Movies & TV
Raelene Boyle	Jun 24, 1951	Sport
Johannes Brahms	May 7, 1833	Classical music
Marlon Brando	Apr 3, 1924	Movies & TV
Rossanno Brazzi	Sep 18, 1918	Movies & TV
Walter Brennan	Jul 25, 1894	Movies & TV
Leonid Brezhnev	Dec 19, 1906	Government
Beau Bridges	Dec 9, 1941	Movies & TV
Jeff Bridges	Dec 4, 1949	Movies & TV
Lloyd Bridges	Jan 13, 1913	Movies & TV
Charles Bronson	Nov 3, 1922	Movies & TV
Charlotte Bronte	Apr 21, 1816	Literature
Emily Bronte	Jul 30, 1818	Literature
Rupert Brooke	Aug 3, 1887	Literature
Elizabeth Barrett Browning	Mar 6, 1806	Literature
Yul Brynner	Jul 11, 1915	Movies & TV
Billie Burke	Aug 7, 1885	Movies & TV
Edgar Rice Burroughs	Sep 1, 1875	Literature
Richard Burton	Nov 10, 1925	Movies & TV
Edd Byrnes	Jul 30, 1933	Movies & TV
Lord Byron	Jan 22, 1788	Literature
Sebastian Cabot	Jul 6, 1918	Movies & TV
James Cagney	Jul 1, 1899	Movies & TV
Erskine Caldwell	Dec 17, 1903	Literature
Taylor Caldwell	Sep 7, 1900	Literature
Maria Callas	Dec 3, 1923	Classical music
Eddie Cantor	Jan 31, 1892	Movies & TV

Al Capone	Jan 17, 1899	Crime
Yvonne De Carlo	Sep 1, 1922	Movies & TV
Art Carney	Nov 4, 1918	Movies & TV
Leslie Caron	Jul 1, 1931	Movies & TV
David Carradine	Dec 8, 1936	Movies & TV
Diahann Carroll	Jul 17, 1935	Movies & TV
Johnny Carson	Oct 23, 1925	Movies & TV
Jimmy (James Earl) Carter	Oct 1, 1924	Government
Enrico Caruso	Feb 25, 1873	Classical music
Casanova	Apr 2, 1725	Paramour
John Cassavetes	Dec 9, 1929	Movies & TV
Fidel Castro	Aug 13, 1926	Government
Catherine the Great	Apr 21, 1729	Royalty
Paul Cezanne	Jan 19, 1839	Painting & Art
Neville Chamberlain	Mar 18, 1869	Government
Richard Chamberlain	Mar 31, 1935	Movies & TV
Raymond Chandler	Jul 22, 1888	Literature
Lon Chaney	Apr 1, 1883	Movies & TV
Carol Channing	Jan 31, 1921	Movies & TV
Charlie Chaplin	Apr 16, 1889	Movies & TV
Geraldine Chaplin	Jul 31, 1944	Movies & TV
Cyd Charisse	Mar 8, 1923	Dancing
King Charles II	May 29, 1630	Royalty
Prince Charles	Nov 14, 1948	Royalty
Anton Chekov	Jan 29, 1860	Literature
Cher	May 20, 1946	Movies & TV
Maurice Chevalier	Sep 12, 1888	Movies & TV
Chiang Kai-Shek	Oct 31, 1887	Government
Frederick Chopin	Feb 22, 1810	Classical music
Agatha Christie	Sep 15, 1890	Literature
Julie Christie	Apr 14, 1941	Movies & TV
Winston Churchill	Nov 30, 1874	Government
Petula Clark	Nov 15, 1932	Movies & TV
Jill Clayburgh	Apr 30, 1944	Movies & TV
Montgomery Clift	Oct 17, 1920	Movies & TV
Lee J. Cobb	Dec 9, 1911	Movies & TV
James Coburn	Aug 31, 1928	Movies & TV
Claudette Colbert	Sep 13, 1907	Movies & TV
Samuel Taylor Coleridge	Oct 21, 1772	Literature

Joan Collins	May 23, 1933	Movies & TV
Ronald Colman	Feb 9, 1891	Movies & TV
Sean Connery	Aug 25, 1930	Movies & TV
Chuck Connors	Apr 10, 1921	Movies & TV
Mike Connors	Aug 15, 1925	Movies & TV
Robert Conrad	Mar 1, 1935	Movies & TV
Jackie Coogan	Oct 24, 1914	Movies & TV
Alistair Cook	Nov 20, 1908	Movies & TV
Terence Cardinal Cooke	Mar 21, 1921	The Church
Alice Cooper	Feb 4, 1948	Popular music
Gary Cooper	May 7, 1901	Movies & TV
Joseph Cotton	May 15, 1905	Movies & TV
Noel Coward	Dec 16, 1889	Theatre
Buster Crabbe	Feb 7, 1908	Movies & TV
Jeanne Crain	May 25, 1925	Movies & TV
Broderick Crawford	Dec 9, 1911	Movies & TV
Joan Crawford	Mar 23, 1904	Movies & TV
Davy Crockett	Aug 17, 1786	Historical
Walter Cronkite	Nov 4, 1916	Television
Bing Crosby	May 2, 1904	Movies & TV
Marie Curie	Nov 7, 1867	Science
Pierre Curie	May 15, 1859	Science
Arlene Dahl	Aug 11, 1928	Movies & TV
Dan Dailey	Dec 14, 1914	Movies & TV
Jim Dale	Jul 15, 1935	Movies & TV
Salvador Dali	Mar 11, 1904	Painting & Art
Linda Darnell	Oct 16, 1923	Movies & TV
Danielle Darrieux	May 1, 1917	Movies & TV
Charles Darwin	Feb 12, 1809	Science
Honore Daumier	Feb 26, 1808	Painting & Art
Marion Davies	Jun 3, 1897	Movies & TV
Bette Davis	Apr 5, 1908	Movies & TV
Miles Davis	May 25, 1926	Popular music
Doris Day	Apr 3, 1924	Movies & TV
Laraine Day	Oct 13, 1920	Movies & TV
James Dean	Feb 8, 1831	Movies & TV
Claude Debussy	Aug 22, 1862	Classical music
Sandra Dee	Apr 23, 1942	Movies & TV

Frederick Delius	Jan 29, 1862	Classical music
Jack Dempsey	Jun 24, 1895	Boxing
Bo Derek	Nov 20, 1956	Movies & TV
Andy Devine	Oct 7, 1905	Movies & TV
Charles Dickens	Feb 7, 1812	Literature
Angie Dickinson	Sep 30, 1931	Movies & TV
Emily Dickinson	Dec 10, 1830	Literature
Marlene Dietrich	Dec 27, 1904	Movies & TV
Phyllis Diller	Jul 17, 1917	Movies & TV
John Dillinger	Jun 22, 1902	Crime
Brad Dillman	Apr 14, 1930	Movies & TV
Joe DiMaggio	Nov 25, 1914	Sport
Walt Disney	Dec 5, 1901	Film Director
Benjamin Disraeli	Dec 21, 1804	Government
Troy Donahue	Jan 27, 1936	Movies & TV
Robert Donat	Mar 18, 1905	Movies & TV
Diana Dors	Oct 23, 1931	Movies & TV
Fyodor Dostoevsky	Nov 11, 1821	Literature
Kirk Douglas	Dec 9, 1916	Movies & TV
Richard Dreyfuss	Oct 29, 1947	Movies & TV
Peter Duchin	Jul 28, 1937	Popular music
Howard Duff	Nov 14, 1917	Movies & TV
Faye Dunaway	Jan 14, 1941	Movies & TV
Isadora Duncan	May 27, 1878	Dancing
Irene Dunne	Dec 20, 1904	Movies & TV
Jimmy Durante	Feb 10, 1893	Movies & TV
Deanna Durbin	Dec 4, 1922	Movies & TV
Robert Duvall	Jan 5, 1931	Movies & TV
Anton Dvorak	Sep 8, 1841	Classical music
Bob Dylan	May 24, 1941	Popular music
Amelia Earhart	Jul 24, 1898	Aviation
Clint Eastwood	May 31, 1930	Movies & TV
Nelson Eddy	Jun 29, 1901	Movies & TV
Barbara Eden	Aug 23, 1934	Movies & TV
Samantha Eggar	Mar 5, 1939	Movies & TV
Albert Einstein	Mar 14, 1878	Science
Dwight D. Eisenhower	Oct 14, 1890	Government
Anita Ekberg	Sep 29, 1931	Movies & TV

Britt Ekland	Oct 6, 1942	Movies & TV
T.S. Eliot	Sep 26, 1888	Literature
Queen Elizabeth I	Sep 1, 1533	Royalty
Queen Elizabeth II	Apr 21, 1926	Royalty
Havelock Ellis	Feb 2, 1859	Medicine
Faye Emerson	Jul 8, 1917	Movies & TV
Ralph Waldo Emerson	May 25, 1803	Literature
Dale Evans	Oct 31, 1912	Movies & TV
Dame Edith Evans	Feb 8, 1888	Movies & TV
Peter Falk	Sep 16, 1927	Movies & TV
King Farouk	Feb 11, 1920	Royalty
Mia Farrow	Feb 9, 1945	Movies & TV
William Faulkner	Sep 25, 1897	Literature
Farrah Fawcett	Feb 2, 1946	Movies & TV
Alice Faye	May 5, 1915	Movies & TV
Fernandel	May 8, 1903	Movies & TV
Jose Ferrer	Jan 8, 1912	Movies & TV
Mel Ferrer	Aug 25, 1917	Movies & TV
Arthur Fiedler	Dec 17, 1894	Classical music
Sally Field	Nov 6, 1946	Movies & TV
Peter Finch	Sep 28, 1916	Movies & TV
Albert Finney	May 9, 1936	Movies & TV
Dietrich Fischer-Dieskau	May 28, 1925	Classical music
Barry Fitzgerald	Mar 10, 1888	Movies & TV
Ella Fitzgerald	Apr 25, 1918	Popular music
Rhonda Fleming	Aug 10, 1923	Movies & TV
Errol Flynn	Jun 20, 1909	Movies & TV
Henry Fonda	May 16, 1905	Movies & TV
Jane Fonda	Dec 21, 1937	Movies & TV
Joan Fontaine	Oct 22, 1917	Movies & TV
Margot Fonteyn	May 18, 1919	Dancing
Glenn Ford	May 1, 1916	Movies & TV
Harrison Ford	Jul 13, 1942	Movies & TV
Steve Ford	May 19, 1956	Movies & TV
Henry Ford II	Sep 4, 1917	Industry
E.M. Forster	Jan 1, 1879	Literature
Connie Francis	Dec 12, 1938	Popular music
Aretha Franklin	Mar 25, 1942	Popular music

Benjamin Franklin	Jan 17, 1706	Government
Sigmund Freud	May 6, 1856	Psychiatry
David Frost	Apr 7, 1939	Movies & TV
William Fulbright	Apr 9, 1905	Government
Clark Gable	Feb 1, 1901	Movies & TV
Eva Gabor	Feb 11, 1924	Movies & TV
Zsa Zsa Gabor	Feb 6, 1920	Movies & TV
Thomas Gainsborough	May 14, 1727	Painting & Art
Mahatma Gandhi	Oct 2, 1869	Crusader
Greta Garbo	Sep 18, 1905	Movies & TV
Ava Gardner	Dec 24, 1922	Movies & TV
Art Garfunkel	Nov 5, 1941	Popular music
Judy Garland	Jun 10, 1922	Movies & TV
James Garner	Apr 17, 1928	Movies & TV
Greer Garson	Sep 29, 1908	Movies & TV
Charles De Gaulle	Nov 22, 1890	Government
Mitzi Gaynor	Sep 4, 1931	Movies & TV
Trevor Howard	Sep 29, 1916	Movies & TV
Rock Hudson	Nov 17, 1925	Movies & TV
Howard Hughes	Dec 24, 1905	Industry
Kim Hunter	Nov 12, 1922	Movies & TV
Walter Huston	Apr 6, 1884	Movies & TV
Barbara Hutton	Nov 14, 1912	Millionairess
Betty Hutton	Feb 26, 1921	Movies & TV
Henrik Ibsen	Mar 20, 1828	Literature
Glenda Jackson	May 9, 1936	Movies & TV
Mick Jagger	Jul 26, 1943	Popular Music
David Janssen	Mar 27, 1930	Movies & TV
Billy Joel	May 9, 1949	Popular music
Elton John	Mar 25, 1947	Popular music
Lyndon Baines Johnson	Aug 27, 1908	President
Van Johnson	Aug 25, 1916	Movies & TV
Al Jolson	Mar 26, 1886	Movies & TV
Jennifer Jones	Mar 2, 1919	Movies & TV
John Paul Jones	Jul 6, 1747	Historical

Shirley Jones	Mar 31, 1934	Movies & TV
Tom Jones	Jun 7, 1940	Popular Singer
James Joyce	Feb 2, 1882	Literature
Carl Gustav Jung	Jul 26, 1875	Psychiatry
Boris Karloff	Nov 23, 1887	Movies & TV
Danny Kaye	Jan 18, 1913	Movies & TV
Sammy Kaye	Mar 13, 1913	Popular music
Buston Keaton	Oct 4, 1895	Movies & TV
Diane Keaton	Jan 5, 1946	Movies & TV
John Keats	Oct 31, 1795	Literature
Howard Keel	Apr 13, 1917	Movies & TV
Brian Keith	Nov 14, 1921	Movies & TV
Sally Kellerman	Jun 2, 1938	Movies & TV
Gene Kelly	Aug 23, 1912	Movies & TV
Edward M. Kennedy	Feb 22, 1932	Government
George Kennedy	Feb 18, 1935	Movies & TV
John F. Kennedy	May 29, 1917	President
Deborah Kerr	Sep 30, 1921	Movies & TV
Frances Parkinson Keyes	Jul 21, 1885	Literature
Prince Aly Khan	Jun 13, 1911	Royalty
Ayatollah Khomeini	May 6, 1900	Religious Leader
Nikita Khrushchev	Apr 16, 1894	Government
Richard Kiley	Mar 31, 1922	Movies & TV
Billy Jean King	Nov 22, 1943	Sport
Martin Luther King	Jan 15, 1929	Political Leader
Dr Alfred Kinsey	Jun 23, 1894	Scientist
Henry Kissinger	Mar 27, 1923	Government
Warner Klemperer	Mar 22, 1920	Classical music
Jack Klugman	Apr 27, 1922	Movies & TV
Andre Kostelanetz	Dec 22, 1901	Classical music
Stanley Kramer	Sep 29, 1913	Movie magnate
Gene Krupa	Jan 15, 1909	Popular music
Alan Ladd	Sep 3, 1913	Movies & TV
Frankie Laine	Mar 30, 1913	Popular music
Hedy Lamarr	Nov 9, 1913	Movies & TV
Dorothy Lamour	Dec 10, 1914	Movies & TV
Burt Lancaster	Nov 2, 1913	Movies & TV

Elsa Lanchester	Oct 28, 1902	Movies & TV
Hope Lange	Nov 28, 1933	Movies & TV
Lillie Langtry	Oct 13, 1853	Actress
Charles Laughton	Jul 1, 1899	Movies & TV
Piper Laurie	Jan 22, 1932	Movies & TV
Peter Lawford	Sep 7, 1921	Movies & TV
D.H. Lawrence	Sep 11, 1885	Literature
T.E. Lawrence	Aug 15, 1888	Lawrence of Arabia
Christopher Lee	May 27, 1922	Movies & TV
Vivian Leigh	Nov 5, 1913	Movies & TV
Jack Lemmon	Feb 8, 1925	Movies & TV
Nikolai Lenin	May 4, 1870	Political Leader
Sam Levene	Aug 28, 1905	Movies & TV
Joseph E. Levine	Sep 9, 1905	Movie Director
Jerry Lewis	Mar 16, 1926	Movies & TV
Jerry Lee Lewis	Sep 29, 1935	Popular music
Sinclair Lewis	Feb 7, 1885	Literature
Beatrice Lillie	May 29, 1898	Actress
Doris Lilly	Dec 26, 1926	Movies & TV
Abraham Lincoln	Feb 12, 1809	President
Charles Lindberg	Feb 4, 1902	Aviator
Sir Joseph Lister	Apr 5, 1827	Medicine
Gina Lollobrigida	Jul 4, 1927	Movies & TV
Carole Lombard	Oct 6, 1908	Movies & TV
Jack London	Jan 12, 1876	Literature
Peter Lorre	Jun 26, 1904	Movies & TV
Bela Lugosi	Oct 20, 1882	Movies & TV
Alfred Lunt	Aug 19, 1892	Movies & TV
Ida Lupino	Feb 4, 1918	Movies & TV
Martin Luther	Nov 10, 1483	Religious Leader
Shirley MacLaine	Apr 24, 1934	Movies & TV
Archibald MacLeish	May 7, 1892	Literature
Fred MacMurray	Aug 30, 1908	Movies & TV
Anna Magnani	Mar 7, 1908	Movies & TV
Gustav Mahler	Jul 7, 1860	Classical music
Norman Mailer	Jan 31, 1923	Literature
Lee Majors	Apr 23, 1942	Movies & TV

Melissa Manchester	Feb 15, 1951	Popular music
Henry Mancini	Apr 16, 1924	Popular music
Joseph Mankiewicz	Feb 11, 1909	Movie Director
Jayne Mansfield	Apr 19, 1933	Movies & TV
Mao Tse-Tung	Dec 26, 1893	Government
Marcel Marceau	Mar 22, 1923	Actor
Frederick March	Aug 31, 1897	Movies & TV
Rocky Marciano	Sep 1, 1924	Boxing
Penny Marshall	Oct 15, 1942	Movies & TV
Dean Martin	Jun 17, 1917	Movies & TV
Mary Martin	Dec 1, 1913	Movies & TV
Tony Martin	Dec 25, 1912	Popular music
Al Martino	Oct 7, 1926	Popular music
Lee Marvin	Feb 19, 1924	Movies & TV
Groucho Marx	Oct 2, 1895	Movies & TV
Harpo Marx	Nov 21, 1893	Movies & TV
Karl Marx	May 5, 1818	Political Leader
James Mason	May 15, 1909	Movies & TV
Pamela Mason	Mar 10, 1918	Movies & TV
Marcello Mastroianni	Sep 28, 1924	Movies & TV
Johnny Mathis	Sep 30, 1935	Popular music
Henri Matisse	Dec 31, 1869	Painting & Art
Walter Matthau	Oct 1, 1920	Movies & TV
Somerset Maugham	Jan 25, 1874	Literature
Virginia Mayo	Nov 30, 1920	Movies & TV
Kevin McCarthy	Feb 15, 1915	Movies & TV
Darren McGavin	May 7, 1922	Movies & TV
Siobhan McKenna	May 24, 1923	Movies & TV
Rod McKuen	Apr 29, 1933	Literature
Ed McMahon	Mar 6, 1923	Movies & TV
Steve McQueen	Mar 24, 1930	Movies & TV
Golda Meir	May 3, 1898	Government
Felix Mendelssohn	Feb 3, 1809	Classical music
Yehudi Menuhin	Apr 22, 1916	Classical music
Melina Mercouri	Oct 18, 1925	Movies & TV
Ethal Merman	Jan 16, 1909	Movies & TV
Michelangelo (Buonarroti)	Mar 6, 1475	Painting & Art
Sarah Miles	Dec 31, 1943	Movies & TV
Ann Miller	Apr 12, 1919	Movies & TV

Henry Miller	Dec 26, 1891	Literature
Hayley Mills	Apr 18, 1946	Movies & TV
Sir John Mills	Feb 22, 1908	Movies & TV
John Milton	Dec 9, 1608	Literature
Yvette Mimieux	Jan 8, 1941	Movies & TV
Sal Mineo	Jan 10, 1939	Movies & TV
Yukio Mishima	Jan 14, 1925	Literature
Robert Mitchum	Aug 6, 1917	Movies & TV
Walter Mondale	Jan 5, 1928	Government
Piet Mondrian	Mar 7, 1872	Painting & Art
Claude Monet	Nov 14, 1840	Painting & Art
Marilyn Monroe	Jun 1, 1926	Movies & TV
Yves Montand	Oct 13, 1921	Movies & TV
Clement Moore	Jul 15, 1779	Literature
Dudley Moore	Apr 19, 1935	Movies & TV
Mary Tyler Moore	Dec 29, 1937	Movies & TV
Roger Moore	Oct 14, 1927	Movies & TV
Jeanne Moreau	Jan 23, 1928	Movies & TV
Rita Moreno	Dec 11, 1931	Movies & TV
Wolfgang Amadeus Mozart	Jan 27, 1756	Classical music
Benito Mussolini	Jul 29, 1883	Dictator
Ogden Nash	Aug 19, 1902	Literature
Patricia Neal	Jan 20, 1926	Movies & TV
Pola Negri	Dec 31, 1894	Movies & TV
Lord Nelson	Sep 29, 1758	Historical
Willie Nelson	Apr 30, 1933	Popular music
Bob Newhart	Sep 5, 1929	Movies & TV
Anthony Newley	Sep 24, 1931	Movies & TV
Paul Newman	Jan 26, 1925	Movies & TV
Sir Isaac Newton	Dec 25, 1642	Science
Wayne Newton	Apr 3, 1944	Movies & TV
Jack Nicholson	Apr 22, 1937	Movies & TV
Florence Nightingale	May 12, 1820	Nursing
Leonard Nimoy	Mar 25, 1931	Movies & TV
David Niven	Mar 1, 1910	Movies & TV
Kim Novak	Feb 13, 1933	Movies & TV
Rudolph Nureyev	Mar 17, 1938	Dancing

Annie Oakley	Aug 13, 1860	Historical
Merle Oberon	Feb 19, 1911	Movies & TV
Hugh O'Brian	Apr 19, 1925	Movies & TV
Margaret O'Brien	Jan 15, 1937	Movies & TV
Pat O'Brien	Nov 11, 1899	Movies & TV
Donald O'Connor	Aug 30, 1925	Movies & TV
Jacques Offenbach	Jun 20, 1819	Classical music
Maureen O'Hara	Aug 17, 1921	Movies & TV
Laurence Olivier	May 22, 1907	Movies & TV
Eugene O'Neill	Oct 16, 1888	Literature
Eugene Ormandy	Nov 18, 1889	Classical music
John Osborne	Dec 12, 1929	Theatre
Peter O'Toole	Aug 2, 1933	Movies & TV
Jack Palance	Feb 18, 1919	Movies & TV
Arnold Palmer	Sep 10, 1929	Sport
Lilli Palmer	May 24, 1914	Movies & TV
Dolly Parton	Jun 19, 1946	Popular music
Louis Pasteur	Dec 27, 1822	Science
Adelina Patti	Feb 19, 1843	Classical music
Les Paul	Jun 9, 1907	Popular music
Pope John Paul II	May 18, 1920	Religious Leader
Pope Paul VI	Sep 26, 1897	Religious Leader
William Penn	Oct 14, 1644	Historical
George Peppard	Oct 1, 1928	Movies & TV
Samuel Pepys	Feb 23, 1633	Historical
Anthony Perkins	Apr 4, 1932	Movies & TV
Oscar Petersen	Aug 15, 1925	Popular music
Pablo Picasso	Oct 25, 1881	Painting & Art
Mary Pickford	Apr 8. 1893	Movies & TV
Molly Picon	Feb 28, 1898	Movies & TV
Gary Player	Nov 1, 1935	Sport
Suzanne Pleshette	Jan 31, 1937	Movies & TV
Christopher Plummer	Dec 13, 1927	Movies & TV
Sidney Poitier	Feb 24, 1920	Movies & TV
Lily Pons	Apr 12, 1904	Classical music
Carlo Ponti	Dec 11, 1913	Movie Director
Ezra Pound	Oct 30, 1885	Literature
Dick Powell	Nov 14, 1904	Movies & TV

Eleanor Powell	Nov 21, 1912	Movies & TV
Tyrone Power	May 5, 1913	Movies & TV
Otto Preminger	Dec 5,1906	Movie Director
Paula Prentiss	Mar 4, 1939	Movies & TV
Elvis Presley	Jan 8, 1935	Popular music
Vincent Price	May 27, 1911	Movies & TV
Louis Prima	Dec 7, 1911	Popular music
Sergei Prokofiev	Apr 23, 1891	Classical music
Juliet Prowse	Sep 25, 1936	Dancing
Anthony Quayle	Sep 7, 1913	Movies & TV
George Raft	Sep 26, 1895	Movies & TV
Tony Randall	Feb 26, 1920	Movies & TV
Raphael (Sanzio)	Apr 6, 1483	Painting & Art
Basil Rathbone	June 13, 1892	Movies & TV
Maurice Ravel	Mar 27, 1875	Classical music
Ronald Reagan	Feb 6, 1911	President
Robert Redford	Aug 18, 1937	Movies & TV
Lynn Redgrave	Mar 8, 1943	Movies & TV
Michael Redgrave	Mar 20, 1908	Movies & TV
Vanessa Redgrave	Jan 30, 1937	Movies & TV
Donna Reed	Jan 27, 1921	Movies & TV
Lee Remick	Dec 14, 1935	Movies & TV
August Renoir	Feb 25, 1841	Painting & Art
Debbie Reynolds	Apr 1, 1932	Movies & TV
Sir Ralph Richardson	Dec 19, 1902	Movies & TV
Diana Rigg	Jul 20, 1938	Movies & TV
Reiner Maria Rilke	Dec 4, 1875	Literature
Tex Ritter	Jan 11, 1907	Movies & TV
Harold Robbins	May 21, 1916	Literature
Cliff Robertson	Sep 9, 1925	Movies & TV
Nelson Rockefeller	Jul 8, 1908	Government
Ginger Rogers	Jul 16, 1911	Movies & TV
Peter Mark Roget	Jan 18, 1779	Literature
Cesar Romero	Feb 15, 1907	Movies & TV
General Rommel	Nov 15, 1891	Military
Mickey Rooney	Sep 23, 1920	Movies & TV
Franklin D. Roosevelt	Jan 30, 1882	President

Philip Roth	Mar 19, 1933	Literature
Georges Rouault	May 27, 1871	Painting & Art
Henri Rousseau	Mar 20, 1844	Painting & Art
Peter Paul Rubens	Jun 29, 1577	Painting & Art
Artur Rubenstein	Jan 28, 1887	Classical music
Dean Rusk	Feb 9, 1909	Government
John Ruskin	Feb 8, 1819	Literature
Jane Russell	Jun 4, 1911	Movies & TV
Lillian Russell	Dec 4, 1861	Movies & TV
Irene Ryan	Oct 17, 1903	Movies & TV
Robert Ryan	Nov 11, 1913	Movies & TV
Dr Albert Sabin	Aug 26, 1906	Science
Francoise Sagan	Jun 21, 1935	Literature
Eva Marie Saint	Jul 4, 1924	Movies & TV
J.D. Salinger	Jan 1, 1919	Literature
Pierre Salinger	Jun 14, 1925	Government
John Singer Sargent	Jan 12, 1856	Painting & Art
George Santayana	Dec 16, 1863	Medicine
Colonel Harlan Saunders	Sep 9, 1890	Business
Telly Savalas	Jan 21, 1925	Movies & TV
Arnold Schoenberg	Sep 13, 1874	Classical music
Franz Schubert	Jan 31, 1797	Classical music
Robert Schumann	Jun 8, 1810	Classical music
George C. Scott	Oct 18, 1927	Movies & TV
Randolph Scott	Jan 23, 1903	Movies & TV
Sir Walter Scott	Aug 15, 1771	Literature
Zachary Scott	Feb 21, 1914	Movies & TV
Neil Sedaka	Mar 13, 1939	Popular music
Erich Segal	Jun 16, 1937	Literature
George Segal	Feb 13, 1934	Movies & TV
Andrés Segovia	Feb 18, 1894	Classical music
Peter Sellers	Sep 8, 1925	Movies & TV
David O. Selznick	May 10, 1902	Movie Director
Doc Sevrinson	Jul 7, 1927	Popular music
Ravi Shankar	Apr 7, 1920	Popular music
George Bernard Shaw	Jul 26, 1856	Literature
Irwin Shaw	Feb 27, 1913	Literature

Norma Shearer	Aug 10, 1905	Movies & TV
Percy Bysshe Shelley	Aug 4, 1792	Literature
Ann Sheridan	Feb 21, 1915	Movies & TV
Dinah Shore	Mar 1, 1917	Movies & TV
Dmitri Shostakovich	Sep 25, 1906	Classical music
Sargent Shriver	Nov 9, 1915	Government
Jean Sibelius	Dec 8, 1865	Classical music
Sylvia Sidney	Aug 8, 1910	Movies & TV
Phil Silvers	May 11, 1912	Movies & TV
Jean Simmons	Jan 31, 1929	Movies & TV
Carly Simon	Jun 25, 1944	Popular music
Frank Sinatra	Dec 12, 1917	Movies & TV
Upton Sinclair	Sep 20, 1878	Literature
Maggie Smith	Dec 28, 1934	Movies & TV
Roger Smith	Dec 18, 1933	Movies & TV
Dick Smothers	Nov 20, 1938	Movies & TV
Suzanne Somers	Oct 16, 1946	Movies & TV
Elke Sommer	Nov 5, 1940	Movies & TV
Ann Sothern	Jan 22, 1909	Movies & TV
John Philip Sousa	Nov 6, 1854	Popular music
Raphael Soyer	Dec 25, 1899	Painting & Art
Dr Benjamin Spock	May 2, 1903	Medicine
Dusty Springfield	Apr 16, 1941	Popular music
Bruce Springsteen	Sep 23, 1949	Popular music
Robert Stack	Jan 13, 1919	Movies & TV
Sylvester Stallone	Jul 6, 1946	Movies & TV
Barbara Stanwyck	Jul 16, 1907	Movies & TV
Gertrude Stein	Feb 3, 1874	Literature
John Steinbeck	Feb 27, 1902	Literature
Saul Steinberg	Jun 15, 1914	Painting & Art
Adlai Stevenson	Feb 5, 1900	Government
Robert Louis Stevenson	Nov 13, 1850	Literature
James Stewart	May 20, 1908	Movies & TV
Rod Stewart	Jan 10, 1945	Popular music
Susan Strasberg	May 22, 1928	Movies & TV
Richard Strauss	Jun 11, 1864	Classical music
Meryl Streep	Jun 22, 1949	Movies & TV
Barbara Streisand	Apr 24, 1942	Movies & TV
Achmed Sukarno	Jun 6, 1901	Government

Barry Sullivan	Aug 29, 1912	Movies & TV
Donald Sutherland	Jul 17, 1934	Movies & TV
Joan Sutherland	Nov 7, 1926	Classical music
Gloria Swanson	Mar 27, 1899	Movies & TV
Algernon C. Swinburne	Apr 15, 1837	Literature
Elizabeth Taylor	Feb 27, 1932	Movies & TV
Rod Taylor	Jan 11, 1930	Movies & TV
Peter Tchaikovsky	May 7, 1840	Classical music
Shirley Temple	Apr 23, 1928	Movies & TV
Margaret Thatcher	Oct 13, 1925	Government
Blanche Thebom	Sep 19, 1919	Classical music
Richard Thomas	Jun 15, 1951	Movies & TV
Terry Thomas	Jul 14, 1911	Movies & TV
Gene Tierney	Nov 20, 1920	Movies & TV
Tiny Tim	Apr 12, 1930	Popular music
Dmitri Tiomkin	May 10, 1899	Classical music
Leo Tolstoy	Sep 9, 1828	Literature
Franchot Tone	Feb 27, 1903	Movies & TV
Mel Torme	Sep 13, 1925	Popular music
Toulouse-Lautrec	Nov 24, 1864	Painting & Art
Spencer Tracy	Apr 5, 1900	Movies & TV
John Travolta	Feb 18, 1954	Movies & TV
Leon Trotsky	Oct 26, 1879	Politics
Pierre Trudeau	Oct 18, 1919	Government
Sonny Tufts	Jul 16, 1911	Movies & TV
Lana Turner	Feb 8, 1920	Movies & TV
William Turner	Apr 23, 1775	Historical
Madame Tussaud	Dec 7, 1761	Historical
Mark Twain	Nov 30, 1835	Literature
Cicely Tyson	Dec 19, 1932	Movies & TV
Liv Ullmann	Dec 16, 1939	Movies & TV
Peter Ustinov	Apr 16, 1921	Movies & TV
Rudy Vallee	Jul 28, 1901	Popular music
Mamie Van Doren	Feb 6, 1933	Movies & TV
Dick Van Dyke	Dec 13, 1925	Movies & TV
Robert Vaughn	Nov 22, 1932	Movies & TV

Giuseppe Verdi	Oct 10, 1813	Classical music
Jules Verne	Feb 8, 1828	Literature
Gore Vidal	Oct 3, 1925	Literature
Pancho Villa	Jun 5, 1878	Literature
Herbert Von Karajan	Apr 5, 1908	Classical music
Max Von Sydow	Jul 10, 1929	Movies & TV
Kurt Waldheim	Dec 21, 1918	Government
Irving Wallace	Mar 19, 1916	Literature
Eli Wallach	Dec 17, 1915	Movies & TV
Jack Warner	Aug 2, 1892	Movie magnate
George Washington	Feb 22, 1732	President
Martha Washington	June 2, 1731	First Lady
Ethel Waters	Oct 31, 1900	Movies & TV
John Wayne	May 26, 1907	Movies & TV
Dennis Weaver	Jun 4, 1924	Movies & TV
Clifton Webb	Nov 19, 1891	Movies & TV
Tuesday Weld	Aug 27, 1943	Movies & TV
Orson Welles	May 6, 1915	Movies & TV
Mae West	Aug 17, 1892	Movies & TV
Dennis Wheatley	Jan 8, 1897	Literature
Gough Whitlam	Jul 11, 1916	Government
Walt Whitman	May 13, 1819	Literature
Richard Widmark	Dec 26, 1914	Movies & TV
Cornel Wilde	Oct 13, 1915	Movies & TV
Oscar Wilde	Oct 16, 1854	Literature
Gene Wilder	Jun 11, 1935	Movies & TV
Emlyn Williams	Nov 26, 1905	Movies & TV
Esther Williams	Aug 8, 1923	Movies & TV
Tennessee Williams	Mar 26, 1911	Literature
Harold Wilson	Mar 11, 1916	Government
Walter Winchell	Apr 7, 1897	Publishing
Duchess of Windsor	Jul 19, 1896	Royalty
Duke of Windsor	Jun 23, 1894	Royalty
Shelley Winters	Aug 18, 1922	Movies & TV
P.G. Wodehouse	Oct 15, 1881	Literature
Thomas Wolfe	Oct 3, 1900	Literature
Natalie Wood	Jul 20, 1938	Movies & TV
Virginia Woolf	Jan 25, 1882	Literature

F.W. Woolworth	Apr 13, 1852	Business
Orville Wright	Aug 17, 1871	Aviator
Wilbur Wright	Apr 16, 1867	Aviator
Jane Wyatt	Aug 12, 1912	Movies & TV
Jane Wyman	Jan 4, 1914	Movies & TV
Keenan Wynn	Jul 27, 1916	Movies & TV
Michael York	Mar 27, 1942	Movies & TV
Susannah York	Jan 9, 1942	Movies & TV
Gig Young	Nov 4, 1913	Movies & TV
Loretta Young	Jan 6, 1913	Movies & TV
Darry F. Zanuck	Sep 5, 1902	Movie magnate
Efram Zimbalist Jnr	Nov 30, 1918	Movies & TV

Bibliography

Addey, J.M. *Harmonics In Astrology* The Camelot Press Ltd, Southampton, 1976

American Astrology Magazine November, 1963

Batra, R. *The Great Depression of 1990* Bantam Books/Schwartz Publishing, Australia, 1985

Davison, R.C. *Astrology* Mayflower Books, London, 1969

Dewey, E.R. and Mandino, O. *Cycles* Manor Books Inc., New York, 1973

Ebertin, R. *The Combination of Stellar Influences* American Federation of Astrologers Inc., USA, 1972

Eysenck, H.J. *Use and Abuses of Psychology* Penguin Books Ltd, England, 1966

Gauquelin, M. *The Truth About Astrology* Hutchinson & Co. (Publishers) Ltd, London, 1984

George, L. *The New A to Z Horoscope Maker and Delineator* Llewellyn Publications, USA, 1985

Gittelson, B. *Biorhythm* Futura Publications Ltd, London, 1978

Goodman, L. *Love Signs* Pan Books Ltd, London, 1980

Goodman, L. *Sun Signs* Pan Books Ltd, London, 1972

Goodwin, M.O. *Numerology, The Complete Guide* Vols 1 & 2, Newcastle Publishing Co., California, 1981

Greene, L. *The Astrology of Fate* Unwin Paperbacks, London, 1985

Greene, L. *Astrology for Lovers* Unwin Paperbacks, London, 1986

Greene, L. *Star Signs for Lovers* Unwin Paperbacks, London, 1980

Hand, R. *Horoscope Symbols* Para Research, Gloucester, Massachusetts, 1985

Hoyle, F. *Ten Faces of the Universe* W.H. Freedman & Co., San Francisco, 1977

Hunt, D. *Exploring the Occult* Pan Books Ltd, London, 1964

Jordan, J. *Numerology, The Romance in Your Name* J.F. Rowny Press, California, 1984

Leoni, E. *Nostradamus and His Prophecies* Bell Publishing Co., New York, 1982

Lindsey, H. and Carlson, C.C. *The Late Great Planet Earth* Bantam Books Inc., USA, 1974

McIntosh, C. *Astrology, The Stars and Human Life: A Modern Guide* Macdonald Unit 75, London, 1970

Nostradamus, *The Prophecies of* Avenel Books, USA

Oken, A. *Astrology: Evolution and Revolution* Bantam Books Inc., USA, 1976

Oken, A. *The Horoscope, The Road and Its Travellers* Bantam Books Inc., USA, 1974

Oken, A. *As Above, So Below* Bantam Books Inc., USA, 1973

Parker, D. & J. *The New Compleat Astrologer* Landsdowne Press, Australia, 1984

Sagan, Carl *Humanist Magazine, Readers Forum* Jan/Feb. 1976

Sepharial *The Manual of Astrology* W. Foulsham & Co.Ltd, London, 1979

Shakespeare, William *Romeo and Juliet* Exeter Books, New York, 1984

Tofler, A. *Future Shock* The Bodley Head Ltd, London, 1972

Turner, C. *The Astrology Book of Calculations* Posh Printing, Australia, 1983

Werfel, F. *Between Heaven and Earth* F. Hubner & Co., New York, 1944

Index